How to make
POLYMER CLAY
Beads

How to make
POLYMER
CLAY
Beads

35 step-by-step projects show how to make beautiful beads and jewelry

LINDA PETERSON

CICO BOOKS
LONDON NEW YORK

First published in 2008 by CICO Books

This edition published in 2013 by CICO Books
An imprint of Ryland Peters & Small Ltd
20–21 Jockey's Fields, London WC1R 4BW
519 Broadway, 5th Floor, New York, NY 10012

www.cicobooks.com

10 9 8 7 6 5 4 3 2

A CIP catalog record for this book is available from the
Library of Congress and the British Library

ISBN: 978 1 906094 44 7
Previous UK ISBN: 978 1 906094 43 0

Printed in China

Editor: Marie Clayton
Designer: David Fordham
Photography: Geoff Dann

For digital editions, visit
www.cicobooks.com/apps.php

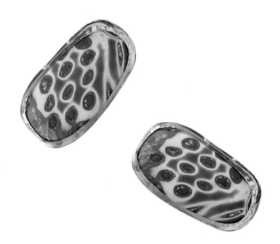

CONTENTS

INTRODUCTION

Imagine, for a moment, you're in a boutique, full of beautiful designer clothing and accessories. A gorgeous beaded necklace catches your eye and you walk over to investigate, only to find that the price is very much out of your budget. Disappointed, you leave the boutique, frustrated and empty-handed. Is this scenario familiar? I'm quite confident that to many of us it is. Well, the next time it happens, turn that scenario into an opportunity to create your own designer jewellery without the enormous price tag. Whether you want to simulate a semi-precious stone, create a complex design inside a cane or maybe just add a touch of whimsy to your wardrobe, this book is for you. And before you say, 'I can't do that,' let me share my story.

I was fortunate enough to grow up in a very creative family. My Dad could create and fix anything. My Mother and Grandmother taught me to sew. My Aunts created mixed media collage art when 'Collage Art' was not yet an art form. My Uncles were musicians and played in various bands. Is it any wonder that I would find myself in a creative profession? Before I began my polymer clay journey – or should I say addiction – I was a stay-at-home mother of two children. To me, crafts or creating anything was a source of stress relief, just a way to relax and wind down. I had a variety of creative hobbies: sewing; jewellery; decorative painting. When I got tired of one, I'd move on to another. However, I put off working with clay, any clay, for a long time even though, like many young children, I had loved modelling clay when I was

a toddler. I would play with it for hours – I didn't really make anything, but I could mix colours and stack shapes. I think I avoided working with clay in my adult years because it scared me. It was okay for a toddler not to make anything, but what if I tried and failed? I believed that somehow I had to take a lifeless blob of clay and miraculously transform it into a work of art.

I began my professional career by accident, after the birth of my daughter, Mariah. She was quite ill and spent most of the first two years of her life in and out of the hospital. I used crafting to pass the time and it drew the interest of the nurses, who would purchase what I made. Soon I was selling at art shows and eventually I began making matching jewellery for the clothing – and this is where I discovered polymer clay. The first time I used it, I was amazed. Actually amazed at a couple of things: first that I created something halfway recognisable and secondly that it wasn't nearly as intimidating as I was anticipating. In fact, it wasn't intimidating at all. It was then that I knew I had to make up for lost time. And so the addiction began!

My designs went from whimsical jewellery to creating whimsical characters, and I developed quite a list of collectors. After several years of travelling to shows, I knew I wanted to teach and share what I knew – I wanted to inspire people. I have now transferred to the design side of the business and I share my knowledge and skills by developing new products for manufacturers, appearing on craft-related

television shows, writing books and teaching workshops all over the world. I don't create as many whimsical characters as in the past, because now my focus is on personal accessories, embellishing everything and creating jewellery.

So why am I sharing all this with you? Because, you may be just like I was: creative… yet afraid to fail. Afraid that you 'just can't do that.' Many times people tell me, 'You make it look so easy!' and I reply, 'That's because it is – let me show you!' I love seeing the look on my student's faces after taking my class and realising 'they just did that!' To a teacher, that is the utmost compliment. Let me reassure you, that there are *no* failures in polymer clay. There are only happy accidents and discoveries. Don't be afraid to make mistakes; mistakes are necessary, learn from them and in this way you will refine your skills.

This book is filled with ideas to get you started on your way to creating your own designer jewellery, just like the items you saw in that boutique. The tips and techniques are there to make this experience a positive one.

I've designed the projects in this technique-based book to suit both beginners and those who are more familiar with polymer clay. I've given careful consideration to ensure they will appeal to a wide range of tastes and styles. Some designs are simple and quick, while others may take a bit more time to master. You may choose to create the projects exactly as they are presented and that is fantastic! However, you may choose to mix and match and throw in a

little of your own personal style, taking the design of one necklace, but using the bead style of another. Whatever you choose and whatever your style, use this book as a stepping stone to create your very own designer jewellery. I hope it will give you inspiration and that you will be able to unleash the creativity that's inside you waiting to jump out. Maybe one day, you'll be one of those designers featured in that boutique.

Enjoy… and prepare for the addiction!

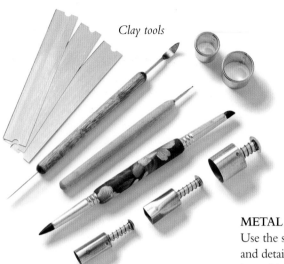

Clay tools

TOOLS

As with any do-it-yourself project, for best results you need to have the right tools. Purchasing quality tools is necessary to achieve professional results and will also help to minimise frustration and make your creative process more enjoyable. Take time to review some of the tools featured here and become familiar with their uses.

CLAY TOOLS
From left to right:

POLYMER CLAY BLADES:
Polyblades come in regular and flexible and are a main staple in my studio. They are extremely sharp and I use them for general cutting and slicing millefiore canes. Always check which is the sharp side before you pick a polyblade up. These blades are not recommended for use by young children and older children should be closely supervised.

TIPS

● *Create a blade cover by rolling a log of clay approximately 5 mm (¼ in.) in diameter. Press the blade into the log and bake. Remove the blade as necessary for projects, placing it back into the cover to protect your fingers when not in use.*

● *Older blades can be sharpened against a piece of sandpaper.*

NEEDLE TOOL AND HOOK COMBINATION:
The needle tool is useful to create dots and designs in your work. I also use it to sculpt with, such as for drawing the veins in leaves. The point will help when setting 'eyes' in your character beads. The hook end is useful to place delicate and tiny pieces onto your project when you are sculpting.

METAL STYLUS:
Use the stylus to impress indentations and details in sculpted beads. This tool is used in the 'Sculpting' chapter of this book and is also very handy to emboss metal.

RUBBER-TIPPED CLAY SHAPER:
This is one of the tools I cannot live without. I use it when sculpting to blend the seams between two joints, by simply 'painting' them – the rubber from the shaper grabs the clay and smoothes the seam. The pointed end is useful to create indentations in the clay, such as holes to take beads for eyes when sculpting.

CLAY CUTTERS:
Available in a variety of shapes and sizes from very small to very large. Some have little springs so that you can punch out the shapes, others are more like a cookie cutter. They are handy to have around, not only for measuring but to create decorative shapes to embellish your designs with.

TIPS

● *Tools that have been taken from the kitchen and used with clay must not be used again for food.*

● *Flatten the clay with a roller before putting it through the pasta machine, to help it pass through the machine easier. Work from the thickest to the thinnest settings.*

PASTA MACHINE
This is another tool that I could not live without. The pasta machine is handy for conditioning clay, rolling out flat sheets and creating a variety of Skinner blends (see page 17). It speeds up conditioning and saves wear and tear on your hands. The dial on the side adjusts the thicknesses of the sheets of clay – typically these range from approximately 2.5 mm (⅛ in.) thick down to paper-thin. To adjust the thickness, pull the dial outwards and twist it to the thickness desired. When the dial is released it should click into place.

Pasta machine

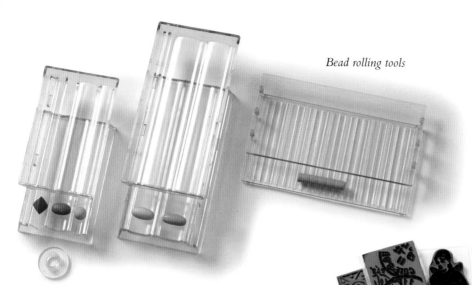

Bead rolling tools

WIRE CUTTERS:
Used to cut wire, eye and head pins. Some are close cut, others cut at an angle. Do not use them to cut memory wire as this will damage the cutting edges – there are special cutters for this wire.

BEAD ROLLING TOOLS
Here are three different types of bead rolling tools. I highly recommend having a set or two since they take the guesswork out of creating perfectly shaped beads, all the same size, quickly and easily. From left to right above: Tri-bead roller; Pro-bead roller; Tube bead roller. See page 14 for bead rolling techniques.

Texturising tools

CLAY BAKING RACK
The bead baking rack is essential for baking beads. The beads can be suspended on a pin, which stops them developing flat spots, and flat pieces can be placed on the bottom. The rack can also be used when slicing canes – place the cane on the acrylic tray and lay inside the rack. Slide the cane to the edge then use a polyblade to slice off even thicknesses of cane. The acrylic tray is also useful to roll logs of even thickness. The pins for baking are the diameter of common bead stringing wire.

TEXTURISING TOOLS
Nearly anything that can create an indentation can be used to texturize clay: an old piece of denim; burlap; wire mesh. Here are a variety of texturing tools, from left: impression tools on wheels, rubber stamps (make sure that they are deeply etched), coarse grit sandpaper, a rock, fibre and a bone folder.

JEWELLERY TOOLS
Basic tools clockwise from left:

NEEDLE-/CHAIN-NOSE PLIERS:
These have tapered half-round jaws. Needle-nose pliers have jagged edges inside, chain-nose are smooth. Use to open and close jump rings and to wrap wire.

ROUND-NOSE PLIERS:
These have tapered jaws and are used to make loops in wire.

CRIMPING TOOLS:
Used to squeeze crimping beads and tubes onto beading wire.

Jewellery tools

Clay baking rack

MATERIALS

There are a variety of materials used throughout this book. Because polymer clay is such a friendly medium, it works well with products such as metallic foils, embossing powders and alcohol-based inks. When trying out a new product, make sure that it will not react with the clay, cause toxic fumes or create a fire hazard.

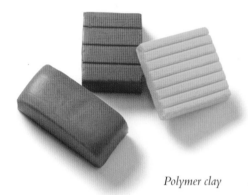

Polymer clay

POLYMER CLAY

Polymer clay is a synthetic clay made from PVC plastic and is available in a variety of brands. It remains soft and pliable until baked in an oven. Each brand has a different feel – some are soft right out of the package, others are a bit stiff. Though the softer clays are easy to work initially, they lack strength after baking. Firmer clays are a favourite among those who create complex designs and are stronger after baking. For the projects in this book, choose a clay that is midway, not too soft and not too firm.

TIPS

● *I work directly on smooth ceramic tiles purchased from the DIY store. They allow you to view your project from different angles and prevent distortion or fingerprints from handling. The clay tile can go directly into the oven for baking.*

● *While the clay is non-toxic and suitable for children, it's a good idea to provide adequate supervision for young children.*

CONDITIONING:

This is vital to the overall strength of your project. You can condition by hand, flattening and twisting until the clay is soft and pliable, but I recommend using the pasta machine. Slice off thin sections of clay and gently flatten with your fingers, then pass the slices through the pasta machine on the thickest setting. Fold the clay in half and repeat until it is smooth and pliable.

BAKING:

Follow manufacturer's instructions for appropriate baking temperatures. I also use an oven thermometer to ensure that you are not baking too hot or too cool. If the clay is burnt, immediately remove it and take it outdoors to cool. Under-baked clay is brittle. Many people use a clay-dedicated toaster oven for baking, which should always be pre-heated. Toaster ovens tend to spike to high temperatures so monitor closely to prevent burning and smelly fumes.

STORAGE:

Okay, so you've made all these great things but you have some leftover clay… now what? Don't throw it away – you can store your clay for a very long time by using zip-lock baggies. You may also use disposable containers – those compatible with polymer clay have a #5 located inside the recycling triangle. Do not let your clay come in contact with styrene plastics (hard plastic, usually transparent) or Styrofoam®. The clay will eat into the surface of these types and cause a huge mess! Keep your clay in a cool, dark area.

TIPS

● *If your clay is too brittle after baking, try using an oven thermometer to ensure you are not baking at too cool a temperature. This will probably solve the problem.*

● *Translucent clays have a tendency to burn easier. Carefully monitor your baking temperatures or reduce the temperature by a couple of degrees.*

OTHER BASIC MATERIALS

Metallic foils, embossing powders, rub on metallic waxes, mica powders, gold and silver leafing sheets and pens, and spices all work well with polymer clay. I also use alcohol-based inks and I've even included peel-off metallic stickers, as a topical surface material. The three items pictured on the lower right-hand corner of the group on page 11 are a selection of adhesives I use when making jewellery. Two-part epoxy provides an exceptionally tight bond between pieces of baked clay or to finish leather cording. Liquid polymer can

TIPS

● *When purchasing clay, make sure it is fresh by slightly squeezing it – don't distort the package, but you should feel a slight give. If the clay is as hard as a rock, don't buy it. Make your clay the last purchase of the day, because leaving it in a car during hot summer months will ruin it – clay begins its curing process at 52°C (125°F).*

● *Always work with the lightest colour first in any of your projects – darker colours will leave a residue on your hands and pasta machine that will contaminate lighter colours. Have baby wipes handy to clean your hands thoroughly between colours.*

Other basic materials, left to right:
Top row – foil sheets, lacquer, metallic wax, gold pen, spices, alcohol-based inks, mica powder.
Bottom row – peel-off metallic stickers, two-part epoxy glue, superglue, double-sided tape.

embosses with a stylus. Pewter contains lead, but can have a protective coating so the lead will not come in contact with your skin. If the lead is of concern, simply apply an additional clear coat of varnish or a very thin coat of liquid polymer over your projects and bake it. An additional option is to apply brass or copper to the back of the pewter.

Pewter and stylus

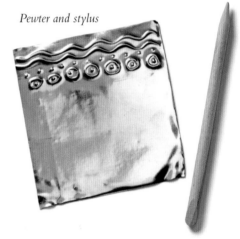

be used for a wide variety of techniques, including binding both baked and raw clay together. It must be baked in order for it to adhere. Cyanoacrilate glues, or superglue (not shown), are an excellent choice for small areas. Double-sided tape is used in the projects here to bind metal to the clay.

METALS

Working with metal is not only fun, but trendy – it adds a touch of bling to your designs. Flat sheets of metal are easy to find in brass, copper, aluminium, coloured aluminium and pewter. My favourite is pewter, which comes in a 23 x 33 cm (9 x 13 in.) sheet. It's very 'creamy' and easily

BASIC JEWELLERY-MAKING MATERIALS

Jewellery components, clockwise from top: jump rings, head pins, eye pins, spacer beads crimp beads, charms, earring wires, selection of rings and beads.

A key to creating beautiful jewellery is not only making lovely beads, but combining them with great accents and findings. You can find a variety of metal spacer beads: some with Swarovski crystals, silver and metal hoops, or decorative charms. You will also need jump rings, eye and head pins, earring loops, clasps and crimp tubes – this list is certainly not all-inclusive!

FINDINGS AND COMPONENTS

A plethora of beads and findings is available on the Internet. For the projects in this book the basics are:

JUMP RINGS:

These attach two components together and can also be used as a design element.

HEAD PINS:

Thin gauge wire with a nail head to prevent beads sliding off. Eye pins have a loop at the end where you can attach additional beads. Both are used for dangles.

SPACER AND METAL BEADS:
These come in a variety of shapes and styles. Base metals provide the look of silver and gold without the cost. Many are non-tarnish and are a good choice for making jewellery.

CLASPS:
Fastenings come in a variety of styles, too many to mention here. I often use toggles and lobster clasps. I love the toggle fastener because its ring and bar adds class and a decorative element. A lobster clasp is a classic choice that is easy to open and close. Attach both the toggle and the lobster clasp with jump rings.

EARRING WIRES:
These are attached to the earring with a jump ring and also come in a variety of styles. The style shown here is most common and is also referred to as the fish hook.

CRIMPING BEADS AND TUBES:
Used with crimp pliers to attach beading wire to a jump ring.

WIRE
I love using wire in my designs because I think it adds an element of interest and flow. I like things that move and by adding wire, you can attach charms and other beads to make your designs more fun. Wire comes in various gauges; the higher the number, the thinner the wire. I've used wire to wrap around

Stringing wire

and embellish beads, as seen in the whimsical and fun coral wire bracelet on page 54. Don't be afraid to experiment!

STRINGING MATERIALS
Beautiful jewellery requires a solid foundation. The type of material you use for stringing is determined by the materials you use and the overall look that you are trying to achieve.

STRINGING WIRE:
This is made of tiny strands all twisted together and is flexible yet strong. The amount of strength is

determined by the number of strands. It comes in a variety of colours, including gold and silver, as well as other styles such as 'crimped' with little zigzags. This adds a very nice decorative touch to your jewellery. Use crimp beads to secure the wire to jump rings or clasps.

Leather cording

LEATHER CORDING:
Whenever I'm creating an ethnic or organic, natural look I tend to incorporate leather cording into the design. You can see that it comes in a variety of colours and widths. Sometimes I use it by itself to accent a focal bead or pendant, other times I use it as a design element to string beads on with a knot to secure.

Wire

FIBRES:

Want to add texture to your design? Fibres are the way to go! They are hot! Recently there has been an explosion of luscious fibres on the market and a great place for them is a specialist knitting shop. Some fibres come with a variety of textures in co-ordinating colours, which helps take out the guesswork. If you tend to use a certain colour palette, buy full skeins of fibres; this can be a little more costly at first, but less expensive in the long run. Don't forget silk or organza ribbons, heavy beading threads and tassels to spice up your designs. I tend to group fibres together and plait to form the overall cord.

CHAINS:

Like movement in your designs? Attracted to dangly jewellery? Chains are the way to go. There are more styles than ever on the market. Thin chains are great to highlight a focal bead. Link chains vary in size and can be used for charm bracelets and necklaces (more movement in design – love it!). Don't be afraid to rip chains apart and use just a small portion as a design element.

Fibres

Other handy materials

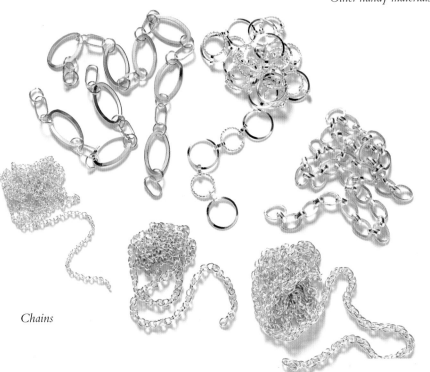

Chains

HANDY MATERIALS TO MAKE YOUR CLAY LIFE EASIER

These are a few staples that I keep around the studio at all times. They include baby wipes, cotton swabs, cocktail sticks, make-up sponges, which are all invaluable.

TECHNIQUES

In this section we cover the basic techniques you will need to work the clay and achieve a wide range of different effects. You can also experiment and find some effects of your own! The basic jewellery techniques will enable you to make your finished beads into some great pieces to wear.

CLAY FORMING TECHNIQUE

None of the tools used in bead making are difficult to use – it's just common sense and practise. And you can make many shapes without any tools at all!

Using bead rollers

Follow the instructions provided with pro-bead rollers on how to measure the right amount of clay. Essentially the process is the same for all, but here I demonstrate the tri-bead roller, the one I use the most.

1 Press a log of clay through the disk to fill the hole, then trim off any excess clay until flush. Press the clay out of the measuring disk with a pencil.

2 The top piece of the roller has a protruding piece on one edge that fits into a groove in the bottom section. Place the clay into a slot, apply the top and slide the two sections back and forth to form your bead.

Bead shapes

With a little manipulation, you can achieve many styles of bead with the rollers; let's talk about some of them. The size of bead depends on the bead roller you are using. For the ones shown here we have used the tri-bead roller.

TOP ROW: The ball, oval and bi-cone are the three original shapes made by using the appropriate measured amount of clay in the bead roller.

SECOND ROW: For a cube, create a ball and use the acrylic tray from the baking rack to flatten all sides.
To make a rectangle, flatten all sides of the oval.
The diamond shaped bead is made by placing extra clay into the bi-cone slot. Use a 'smash and rock' technique to flatten the bead, but not roll it completely over. This usually puts little tabs onto the side of the bead, which can be trimmed off.

THIRD ROW: For the disk, flatten the ball and poke a hole.
To make the flattened oval, flatten the oval with the acrylic tray.

BOTTOM ROW: For a puff bead, add extra clay to the oval slot and gently 'smash and rock'. The bead will not roll completely over but will spread out to form this shape.

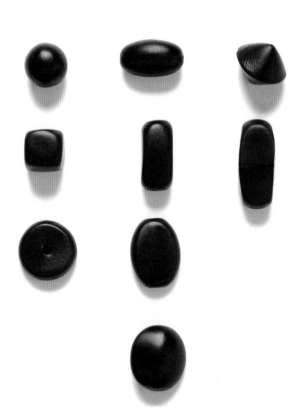

Hand-forming beads

These pictures show a couple of different ways that you can hand-form your beads. Beads that are hand-formed will naturally vary in shape and size, unlike those made in a roller. The nice thing about this technique is there is absolutely no measuring involved!

TIPS

● *Never throw any scrap clay away! You can use it as the inside of larger focal beads, then wrap the outside with the desired base colour to save on 'good' clay.*

● *Keep in mind that once it is wrapped, the final bead will likely be larger than expected. The solution to this is to start out with a smaller base bead than you feel is necessary.*

1 Use the various parts of your hand to gently shape the bead into the desired form. You many find yourself distorting one area while working on another.

2 It is a good idea to work a little and then refine a little. Hand-formed beads are used to create some of the simulated stone techniques on pages 26–75.

Here are some examples of the many different shapes and sizes you can achieve by hand. Get creative!

Creating the bead holes

If you want to thread your beads, you will need to create a hole through the centre before you bake them.

TIP

● *Clay artist Dottie McMillian, suggests inserting eyelets into the hole to give them a finished look. This will help to reduce the possibility of any abrasion around the hole when working with some stringing materials.*

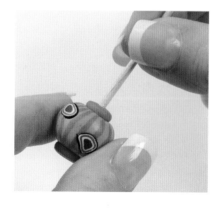

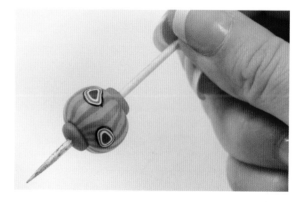

1 Gently hold the bead between your thumb and forefinger. With a twisting motion, much like a drill, gently press the cocktail stick through the centre of the bead, just until it begins to poke out the other side.

2 Remove the cocktail stick carefully and insert it again from the other side, into the exact spot where it was poking through. This will give you a nice finished hole on both sides of your bead.

CLAY MIXING

Polymer clay comes in many colours, but don't limit yourself to just the colours provided. You can mix any colour under the sun by following a few guidelines. It is a good idea to invest in a colour wheel since this will help you in mixing just the perfect colour for your project. If you only want to purchase a few colours in the beginning, then I would suggest primary colours along with black and white. The primary colours make up the basis to create all other colours. Simply put, red and blue make purple, blue and yellow make green and so on. You can also create various tints and shades by adding amounts of white and black. Sometimes you may feel that a colour is just too bright. Dull the colour down by mixing in small amounts of the colour opposite on the wheel. You will not change the colour, but it will be muted. Keep mixing in the opposite colour until the desired effect is achieved. You can also make swatches of your own colour wheel for future use.

While we are on the subject of mixing, let's talk about a few of the things that you can 'mix-in' or add to the clay to create variations, patterns and effects in the clay. Creating these beads is a great way to begin since you are only working with one colour.

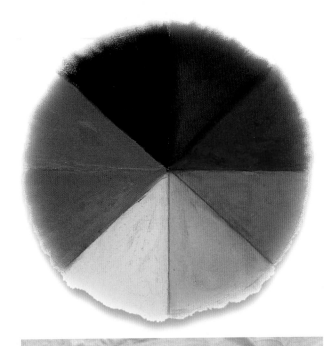

TIP
● *Sometimes you get streaks or specks of another colour in your clay. Not to worry! Keep on blending and soon that unwanted colour will quickly disappear – so long as there is not a significant amount of it.*

Embossing powders, both inside and topical, create speckled effects. Rub-on metallic waxes and mica powders will highlight raised areas that have been created by impressing a pattern or texture into the clay. Paint with brown onto a tan bead for a wood effect.

Glitter on top or mixed into the clay will add bling! Spices add a natural feel to your beads. Paint polka dots in a contrast colour onto a plain base bead for a simple yet whimsical effect. Texturise colour with a sponge and ink for an organic feel.

TIPS
● *Make sure that the elements you mix into the polymer clay are compatible with it and are suitable for baking, so they will not cause toxic fumes or burn.*

● *For colours you use often, create a swatch with a hole on one corner and bake. Write the mixing recipe on the back and keep on a key ring for reference.*

Marbling

Marbling can be done by hand and in the pasta machine. Both start in the same way, by rolling two or more colours into logs. Twist the logs together. Fold in half and twist, repeating this process until the desired marble effect is achieved. When marbling through your pasta machine, twist logs together and roll through the thickest setting on the pasta machine. Fold in half and roll. Repeat these steps until you achieve the desired marble effect.

Skinner blends

Skinner blends, named after Judith Skinner who developed the technique, are a favourite among polymer clay artists. I would consider this a 'staple' technique – one that everyone should know. The possibilities with this technique and its variations are endless. Let's take a look at the basic Skinner blend, which forms the basis for several of the projects featured.

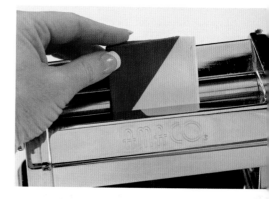

1 Select two colours – complementary or contrasting. Flatten the clay on the thickest setting of the pasta machine and cut two right angle triangles the same size. Place the triangles together, offsetting them slightly and forming a rectangle. Clip off the little triangular tags at the edge. Offsetting the triangles allows pure colour to remain on both sides of the blend.

2 Pass the two-colour rectangle through the pasta machine, using the thickest setting. Note that the pure colour is on each side of the blend. Roll through the pasta machine, keeping the sheet running in the same direction each time.

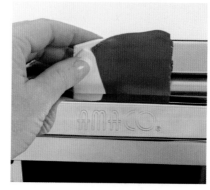

3 Fold the clay each time so that the colour on the sides matches. In this case we have a purple side and a white side. Place the fold along the rollers and roll through the pasta machine again.

4 Continue this process until your blend is smooth. Generally this takes around 15-20 passes through the pasta machine.

5 When finished you should have a nice blended sheet. Pass the blended sheet white end first through the second thinnest setting on the pasta machine to elongate the sheet. You can then use it as a laminate for a bead or as a basis for several variations.

CREATING BASIC CANES AND 3-D SHAPES

Canes are long lengths of clay that are used both as beads themselves and to create a length of design – that runs through the middle of the cane – which you can slice off and apply to your beads. Experiment, as patterns can look quite different in different sizes. The 3-D shapes can be created by using moulds or with my simple sculpting techniques on page 21.

Bull's-eye cane

The bull's-eye cane creates circles of concentric colour to decorate your beads. See the reducing canes technique on page 20 to make the circles in varying sizes. For several sizes of the same design, roll only one side of the cane smaller.

1 Wrap a medium-thick sheet of black clay around a tan clay log.

2 Trim off the excess wrap. Match the seam and smooth together.

3 Slice circles from the cane to decorate your beads.

4 You may keep applying different colour layers to create additional variations of this cane.

TIPS

● *Create variations to this cane by simply mixing up the order of the layers or by adjusting the thickness of the layers. You can also alter the shape from round to triangular. Adding a final thin wrapping layer of black will give your canes definition.*

● *Allow canes to sit and rest for a while after making them. I know it's so much fun to see the 'reveal' but your patience will pay off, because allowing the cane to rest will result in much less distortion of the pattern during the reduction process.*

Basic jellyroll or spiral cane

This cane has a spiral of two colours running through it. Again, see reducing techniques on page 20 to make the cane different thicknesses.

1 Flatten two sheets of clay through the pasta machine on a medium thickness. Stack the sheets on top of one another. Remove any air bubbles by passing the stack back through the pasta machine on a thick setting. Then roll the stack up into a cane.

2 Roll the stack between your fingers to make a nice smooth and even log.

3 Roll the cane from one end to the other to reduce it in diameter and increase it in length.

4 If you roll the cane thinner at one end, you will have a selection of different size circles to work with.

Basic stripes

It's so easy to make stripes in clay – just stack and slice!

1 Run two colours through the pasta machine on a medium setting. Stack the sheets in alternating colours. Cut the stack into four equal sections and stack again. Slice off thin sections and pass through the pasta machine.

2 Work down to the thinnest. Do not skip settings as this will tend to crack and obscure the strips. Cut a section and wrap your base bead.

3 Smooth the ends of the wrapping onto the bead at the top and the bottom, working evenly round so the strips converge neatly into the centre. Make a new threading hole through the wrapping.

4 Roll the striped bead between your fingers so the covering is firmly attached. Bake the bead.

Skinner blend roll

Start by creating the Skinner blend sheet as described on page 17.

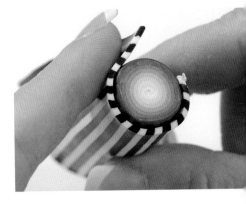

1 Working at one end, roll up towards the opposite end as if you were creating a jellyroll.

2 The finished cane has an even colour gradation from light to dark – or you can reverse and have dark to light.

3 Cut a 2.5-mm (⅛-in.) thick slice from striped cane and wrap it around the Skinner blend roll.

Reducing canes

Generally it is necessary to reduce the pattern inside the cane for your project. I have shown basic canes – the more complex the cane, the bigger you need to make at the start to show detail and the more patience you will need when reducing. Now you know why I do simple canes! I love instant gratification!

1 Begin by simply warming the cane in your hands. This will prevent cracks appearing in the clay. Gently press from the centre outward. Working your way to the ends of the clay. Be gentle!

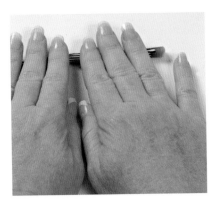

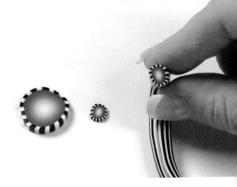

2 Gently roll the clay back and forth to smooth the log. You can slice the cane in half if it is easier to reduce using smaller sections of log.

3 Rotate the cane to the opposite side to ensure that you are reducing with even pressure (typically we are stronger on one hand than the other).

4 When the desired size has been reached, slice off thin sections and apply to your beads. You can roll the beads so that the canes are flush with the surface or you can leave them as is for a more appliquéd look.

Creating moulds from found objects

Creating moulds from objects is a great way to reproduce them in a variety of ways. There are mould kits available on the market but you can create your own moulds easily and without the added expense just by using your scrap clay. Anything you can press into the clay can be moulded. Think of buttons, chains, leaves – anything that will leave an impression and give you an interesting pattern.

1 Condition the clay (I use scrap clay for my moulds) and roll into a ball. Spray the item to be moulded with water for easy release. Press the item down into the ball. Make sure that the clay fills all the grooves to get a good impression.

2 If the item being moulded is bakable you may bake it inside the mould. If not, gently pull the mould back and remove it. Bake the mould in the oven for 30 minutes and allow to cool.

3 Here you can see the original item, the mould and the replica! Pretty cool!

General sculpting and the Six Simple Shape™ technique

If you can break an object down to its most basic forms and build from there, you will have mastered the Six Simple Shape™ technique. You'll get more practise in the sculpting chapter of this book.

BALL: This is the basis for all other shapes. Balls in various sizes can become toes, for instance, or scales on fish or alligators – you get the idea.

LOG: The log forms the basis for the tapered log and is used in jewellery.

TAPERED LOG: Apply more pressure to one side to get the thin end. Tapered logs and variations are used a lot for arms and legs.

TEARDROP: Round the thick end of the tapered log. These are useful in making ears for animals, like a rabbit.

CONE: The cone is the shape that I use the most for the body.

SQUARE OR CUBE: I use this less frequently and mostly for embellishment.

FINISHING TECHNIQUES

When you have made your beads or other shapes and baked them, you may want to add different finishes for even more variations. There are several types of finish, the ones I use the most are detailed here.

Antiquing

Antiquing your beads is a wonderful way to highlight all the beautiful impressions – and sometimes imperfections – in the surface, giving them age and character.

> **TIP**
> ● *If the paint is stubborn and hard to remove, wet a make-up sponge with rubbing alcohol. This will make the paint remove rather easily. For those really tough spots where it's hard to sand, gently scrape away any unwanted paint.*

1 Paint the baked bead entirely with acrylic paint and allow it to dry thoroughly.

2 Sand away the paint on the surface of the bead, leaving some paint in the cracks and crevasses to highlight the design.

Sanding

Sanding your project by hand is very hard work, but well worth the results. While I'm removing the paint during the antiquing process, I am also beginning to sand the surface smooth at the same time. Here I have used 400 grit wet/dry sandpaper to begin with. Continue sanding the surface and increasing your grit from 600, 800, 1000 and up to 1500. After this, the clay should feel satin smooth and you can then choose one of the buffing or varnishing options to complete the look.

The buffing process will highlight any unwanted imperfections, but you can just go back and sand only that area – increasing the grit as you go – to remove the imperfection. Then you will have to re-buff that area to match the rest.

> **TIPS**
> ● *For those areas that are exceptionally rough, you may start with a coarser grit of 320. However, be very careful not to sand your design away completely at this stage. Move onto finer sandpaper as soon as you can.*
>
> ● *When sanding, use wet/dry sandpaper available online or from car parts stores. Have a bowl of water handy and a drop of soap. The soap prevents build-up of clay particles on the sandpaper. The water helps you to keep from breathing the dust. If in doubt you may need to wear a dust mask.*

Buffing

After sanding, many artists choose to apply either a matt finish or a glossy one.

To achieve the glossy effect, simply buff the bead using a buffing wheel – you can use a grinding wheel fitted with a muslin polishing wheel. Alternatively, a jewellery-buffing lathe is also ideal, although it is a more expensive choice. These machines significantly speed up the process of bringing the clay to a glass-like shine, and may be a good choice for you if you need a break from the hard work of sanding. If you are happy to buff by hand, hunt through your old jeans – all you need is a small piece of denim for buffing to a matt finish.

If neither of these options works for you, go the quick and easy route – see varnishing!

1 For a satin matt finish, buff the bead on a piece of old denim.

Varnishing

The easiest way to get a quick gloss is to paint the surface with a gloss varnish, but make sure that it is compatible with the clay. A sealer is not always necessary, but you can use one to protect the surface, especially if you have applied surface treatments such as paint or foil that are lying on top of the clay.

TIP
● *A simple piece of packing foam makes a great drying rack when you are varnishing. Simply poke the cocktail stick into the threading hole of the bead and push the other end into the foam. This allows the beads to dry without touching anything or marking.*

BASIC JEWELLERY-MAKING TECHNIQUES

To make your beads into jewellery you will need a few jewellery-making techniques – but nothing too complex!

Using jump rings

Using crimp beads

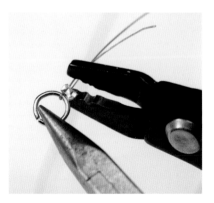

1 Use pliers to twist the jump ring apart to open. Twist in the opposite direction to close. Do not pull jump rings apart.

1 Thread a crimp bead or tube onto beading wire. Place the end of the wire through a jump ring and thread back through the crimp bead.

2 Place the crimp bead close to the jump ring. Squeeze the crimp bead with crimping pliers to secure to the wire.

CHAPTER 1

Simulating Stone Effects

When I want to simulate a certain
type of stone, I use beading catalogues for
reference or take a trip to the bead shop.
I love to look at the detail on each bead and
work out the recipe for it in my mind.
The process of learning how to mimic real
semi-precious stones is fascinating and it is very
gratifying to create that look from
a lifeless block of clay. Many times it can take
hours or even a couple of days to fine tune the
recipe, but you don't have to waste any time
getting started because these recipes are easy to
follow. The projects are designed to teach
techniques and once you've mastered those…
well, the sky's the limit!

FOREVER AMBER

Golden amber is a timeless natural material that has been formed over the centuries from tree sap. These glorious beads look just like true antiques – who will know you only made them yesterday! Keep your amber beads fairly chunky, just like the real thing.

MATERIALS

Polymer clay: Classic Translucent,
Sunflower Yellow,
Mandarin Orange, Caramel

Pasta machine

Polyblade

Bead baking tray

Grit and dirt

Burnt Umber acrylic paint

Cocktail stick

400 and 600 grit sandpaper

Wet wipe

Beading wire

Two 8 mm silver spacer beads

Twenty-three 3 mm silver spacer beads

Forty-four 3 mm silver roundels

Two jump rings

Two crimp beads

Length of small link chain

Toggle fastener

Stretch cord

Necklace

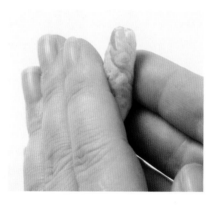

1 Chop 2 parts Classic Translucent, 1 part Suflower Yellow, a pea-size ball of Mandarin Orange and a pinch of Caramel into small pieces. Taking a small lump of mixed clay, gently roll into a log.

2 Twist the colours so that they swirl. Fold in half and roll into a log again. What you should end up with is yellow clay with very faint swirl lines in it. Roll into a 1.5-cm (¾-in.) log and slice off 1-cm (½-in.) sections.

3 Create round and oval beads as desired, forming them between your fingers. They can be slightly lumpy, like natural amber chunks. Press in dirt and grit for texture and create a threading hole, as described on page 15.

FINISHING

Bake all the beads according to manufacturer's baking instructions and allow to cool. Paint over the beads with Burnt Umber acrylic paint, then use a fine grit sandpaper to sand away the paint, leaving it only in the cracks on the surface. To keep the beads in the natural state, I only sand to 600. Apply a satin finish by buffing on denim.

ASSEMBLING

For an approximately 46-cm (18-in.) choker, attach beading wire to a jump ring with crimp beads, string on a 3 mm spacer, 8 mm spacer, 3 mm roundel, amber bead, roundel, 3 mm spacer. Add the remaining amber beads with a roundel-spacer-roundel in between each bead. Finish with 8 mm spacer and 3 mm spacer with a jump ring. Attach a 7.5-cm (3-in.) piece of chain to each jump ring. Attach a toggle to one jump ring. Adjust the length of the necklace by adjusting the length of the chain.

Bracelet

Measure the wrist and add 7.5 cm (3 in.). Cut stretch cord to the measured length and tie a large knot in one end. String on amber beads as desired, with spacer beads in between. Tie both ends together and hide the knot inside one of the beads.

BURNT SIENNA BEADS

The rich tan of these curved cinnabar tube beads brings to mind visions of rolling terracotta sand dunes. The cool silver spacer beads add an ethnic look that is right up to date. The cinnabar mix is just so easy to make.

MATERIALS

Polymer clay: Indian Red, Black
Tube bead roller
Drinking glass
Craft knife
Fantasy fibre (fine hair-like fibres)
Cocktail sticks
Black acrylic paint
Make-up sponge
320 to 400 grit sandpaper
Beading wire
Two crimp beads
Sixteen 2 mm silver bead caps
Nine silver spacer beads
Lobster clasp
Length of chain

PREPARATION

The basic cinnabar mix is a combination of Indian Red and Black. Both are very pigmented colours. Mix 5 parts Indian Red to 1 part Black – you only want to darken the shade of the red colour. This choker is around 40.5 cm (16 in.) long – add more beads if a longer length is desired.

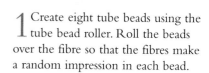

1 Create eight tube beads using the tube bead roller. Roll the beads over the fibre so that the fibres make a random impression in each bead.

FINISHING

Paint the beads with Black acrylic paint and allow to dry. Sand with 400 grit sandpaper until smooth, leaving the paint only in the surface cracks. Apply sealer if desired.

ASSEMBLING

Attach a 46-cm (18-in.) piece of beading wire to a jump ring with a crimp bead. Trim the end of the wire to 1 cm (½ in.). Thread on a spacer bead, 2 mm bead cap, tube bead, bead cap, then a spacer bead. Repeat this order until the necklace is complete. Finish with a crimping bead, hiding the end of the beading wire inside the beads. Add chain and clasp.

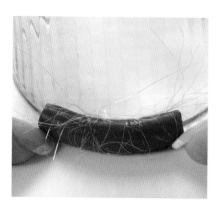

2 Shape beads into a curve by moulding them around the base of a drinking glass, then bake.

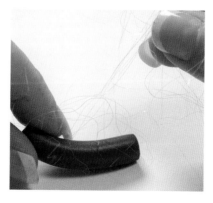

3 After cooling, pull away the fibres and sand away the residue with 320 grit sandpaper.

ORIENTAL SEAL PENDANT

Evoke the mystery of the Orient with this gorgeous Chinese-style cinnabar pendant. The original object used to make a mould for the piece shown here was one of a series of interesting seals, which I bought in Chinatown. Keep a look out for interesting textures and unusual designs for future use.

MATERIALS

Polymer clay: Indian Red, Black
Spray bottle of water
Mould of a found object
Light bulb
Black acrylic paint
400, 600 and 800 grit sandpaper
Two eye pins
Tube bead roller
Jump ring
Cocktail stick
61-cm (24-in.) length of leather cording

1 Spray the mould with water before you start. Flatten a sheet of clay on the thickest setting and impress into the mould.

2 Gently lift the clay shape from the mould, being careful not to distort the shape. Trim off the excess clay around the edge.

3 Place the moulded clay onto a light bulb to get the convex shape and refine, trimming away any extra clay. Repeat the last three steps for the reverse side.

4 Bake both pieces on the light bulb, following the clay manufacturer's instructions. After cooling, apply superglue to the edges of one side of the moulded clay.

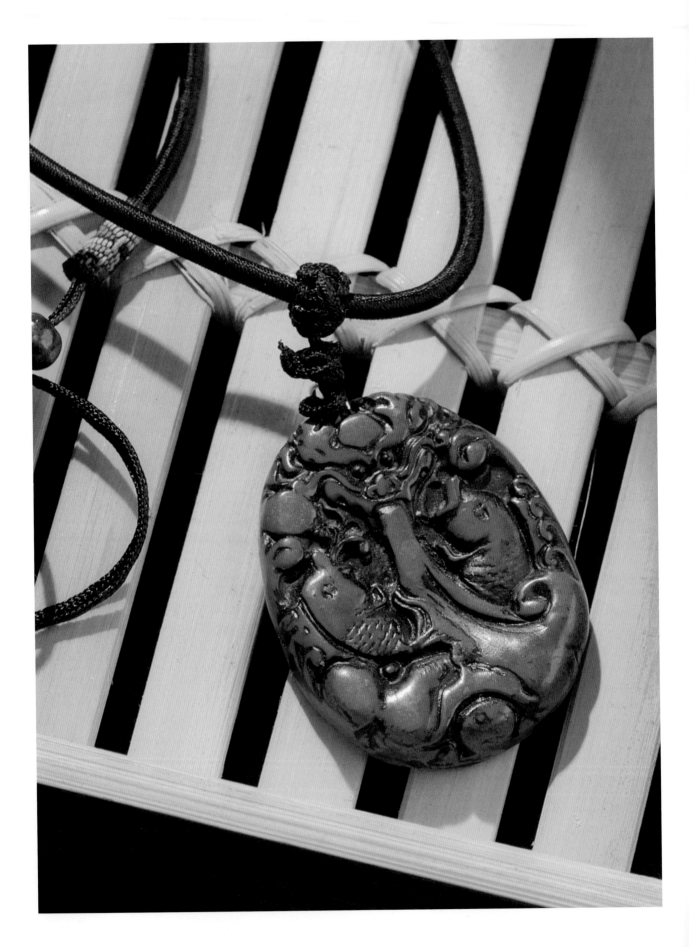

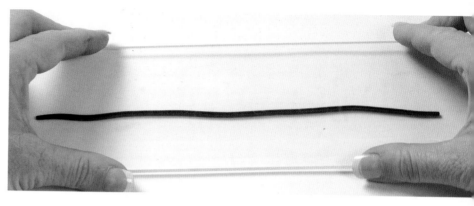

5 Place the other half on top and allow the glue to set.

6 Take some plain Black clay and roll out a very long, thin log, using the acrylic tray from your clay baking rack to keep it an even thickness.

7 Wrap the log around the seam between the two halves of the focal bead to hide the join. Trim the ends flush and press in place, then re-bake the entire bead.

8 Paint across the surface of the pendant with Black acrylic paint, using a sponge to work some of the paint into the lines and crevices of the design.

9 Sand away some of the paint with 400 grit sandpaper. Continue sanding, increasing the grit to make the surface soft and smooth. Apply sealer. Decide where the top of your focal pendant is and drill a small hole for the eye pin. Glue in the eye pin.

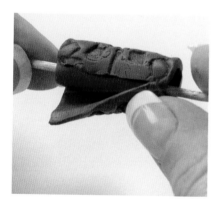

11 Smooth the seam. Trim an eye pin to 1 cm (½ in.) and insert into the centre of the tube bead. Make an oval bead with a textured surface. Bake, antique and sand the tube bead and oval bead as for the focal pendant. Attach the focal pendant to the tube bead with a jump ring.

TIP
● *Glue all the knots after you have made them. Then there is no chance they will come undone when you cut the cord close to the knot to neaten the ends off.*

10 Create a tube bead using the tube bead roller. Repeat the steps for creating the texture in the mould, cut a square of the design and wrap around a cocktail stick.

ASSEMBLING
Insert leather cording through the hole in the tube bead and knot on each side of the bead. Create a loop at one end big enough for the oval bead, and tie the oval bead onto the other end. Thread the oval bead through the loop to close the necklace.

WHITE MARBLE NECKLACE

Each time I wear this jewellery, I get loads of compliments. If you asked me
what was my favourite technique I would have a hard time narrowing it down
to just one – but this would definitely be among my top 10.
The marble technique, while so simple to do, can look so different depending on
the colours of clay and paint that you choose.

MATERIALS

Polymer clay: White, Classic
Translucent
Black acrylic paint
Paint brush
Polyblade
Scrap clay
Pro-bead roller #1 (optional)
Round circle cutter or small tin
Small circle cutter
Sandpaper
Gloss varnish
Thirteen small silver spacer beads
Seven eye pins
Chain with large links
Clasp
Stretch cord
Ten medium silver spacer beads

TIPS

● *The bead rollers are handy to
create base beads that are all the
same size.*

● *At first, I thought it would be
good to paint the pieces just before
I left the studio the night before so
they had all night to dry and
I wouldn't be impatiently waiting.
However, when I returned the next
day the paint had reacted with the
clay – you have about 4–5 hours
after the paint dries before this
happens. It's best to paint the clay
only an hour or so before you need
to use it. If it begins to get a little
sticky, dust your hands with some
baby powder.*

Necklace

PREPARATION
Create several base beads from scrap
clay using one of the bead rollers or
hand-roll them. Roll more than you
think you will need, the extras always
come in handy.

Mix equal parts of white and
translucent clay. You do not have to
completely mix the clay, it is good to
have some of the translucent and
pure white showing. Roll up into a
ball and slightly flatten.

1 Chop the prepared clay into small pieces using the polyblade. Notice the
range of sizes in the pieces, you want some to be small, medium and large.

2 Paint all the pieces with Black paint. Make sure they are completely covered. Allow to dry; this may take up to an hour.

3 After the paint has dried, roll the chopped pieces into a ball and slice thin slices off to apply to a round base bead.

4 Repeat on the other round base beads. Shape some of the round beads into square beads between your fingers.

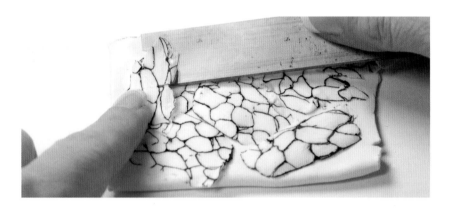

5 To create the focal pendant, flatten a sheet of white clay to the thickest setting on the pasta machine. Cut slices from the marble clay as thin as possible and apply them to the white sheet in a pleasing pattern.

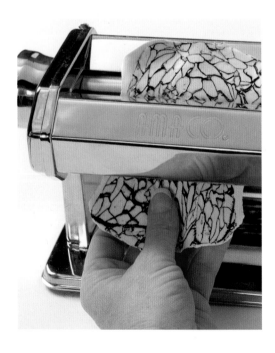

6 Roll the finished sheet through the pasta machine again to smooth the surface. Lay the sheet out on a flat surface to cut out the shapes.

7 I've used a round tin as the basis for my circle. Press the tin into the clay to cut the circle out. If using a template, cut the circle using a craft knife.

8 Cut out the centre of the disc with the small circle cutter. Make a little hole in the top of the pendant with a cocktail stick to insert the eye pin.

9 Make threading holes in the beads, then bake all the beads and the focal pendant. Sand the surface of the pendant and beads to smooth and remove any smear marks.

ASSEMBLING

Thread a small silver spacer bead onto the eye pin, thread on the marble bead, another spacer bead, then twist the wire into a loop as shown on page 115. Repeat for all the marble beads. Cut the last eye pin down to 5 mm (¼ in.) in length, thread a small silver spacer bead onto it and glue into the hole in the focal pendant. Attach the beads between lengths of chain using jump rings and following the photograph as a guide. Hang the focal pendant in the centre with a jump ring.

TIPS

● *If you plan to work with clay a lot, kitchen equipment such as a food processor and the pasta machine are great for chopping, mixing and conditioning clay. However you must have dedicated equipment just for your clay.*

● *You can also make black marble beads using this same technique. Follow the above instructions, but use black clay and grey paint instead, to create a different look.*

● *Many different natural stones have other colours running through them like this and it is hard to get fine lines of another colour using two colours of clay. With this chopping and painting technique the possibilities are endless!*

Bracelet

1 Measure your wrist and add 5 cm (2 in.). String about ten of the marble beads on with a medium silver spacer bead between each. Knot the stretchy cord to secure and hide the knot inside one of the beads.

MOONSTRUCK

A glowing moon is something essentially romantic but mysterious – just like the gleaming beads I have created for this glorious necklace. The large links of the chain echo the shape of the beads and the Swarovski crystals and glass drops flash like diamonds.

MATERIALS

Polymer clay: Classic Translucent, Leaf Green Classic

Ground herbs, such as mixed spice

Rubber stamp or texture of choice

Light bulb

Sandstone acrylic paint

Make-up sponge

400 grit sandpaper or light sanding sponge

24-gauge non-tarnish silver wire

Superglue

Gloss varnish

Chain with large links

Six square links with Swarovski crystals

Six glass teardrop beads

Seven 3 mm round spacer beads

Two earring wires

Toggle fastener

Necklace

PREPARATION

Jade ranges from light green to yellow so the mix you create needs to have some of these colour variations. Therefore it isn't necessary to be precise when measuring. I would suggest that you make extra clay each time you make a batch of jade – the colour variations tend to make the jade look more realistic.

1 The mix contains mostly Translucent – mix 1 part Translucent to a pea-size ball of Leaf Green. Adjust the intensity of the green by adding more Leaf Green colour. Add herbs on top of a flat layer of green clay. Mix the herbs into the clay by folding and rolling through the pasta machine. Flatten to the thickest setting on the pasta machine. Create texture with a stamp. Cut out 14 circles in the desired size, using a template or a circle cutter. Place the circles onto a light bulb, trim any rough edges with a craft knife.

ASSEMBLING

Add a round spacer bead to the top of each wire and create a loop. Trim off any excess clay. Thread a short length of wire through one side of a square link, add a crystal teardrop bead at the bottom, then thread the wire up the other side. Twist the two ends of wire together at the top, then form a loop with one end before twisting it around to secure. Snip off any excess wire. Attach six of the square links and five of the beads to the chain, alternating them as shown.

2 Bake the circles. When cool, apply paint, allow to dry and sand off. Curl a 7.5-cm (3-in.) piece of wire into a spiral and place in the middle the clay disk. The spiral will stop the wire from pulling out when the two halves of the bead are glued together.

3 Apply superglue around the perimeter of the bottom bead. Place the second half of the bead on top, sandwiching the wire in place. Hold together for a few seconds until set. Repeat for the remaining disks. Varnish the finished beads.

CHINESE WHISPER CHAIN

The thing about Chinese whispers is that the message changes very slightly as it is passed down the line – and these hand-stamped beads are all slightly different, which adds to their charm. The mix for this necklace is slightly darker than that used on the Moonstruck necklace, you can adjust the colour to fit your personality.

MATERIALS

Polymer clay: Classic Translucent, Classic Leaf Green

Pro-bead roller set #2 (12 mm and 24 x 11 mm oval)

Rubber stamp with texture of choice

Cocktail stick

Burnt Umber and Sandstone acrylic paint

Make-up sponge

400 grit sandpaper or sanding sponge

22-gauge non-tarnish silver wire

Twenty-two 4 mm flat spacer beads

Twenty-two 4 mm spacer beads

Twelve jump rings

Clasp

1 Make up the jade mix to your desired colour and create 7 oval and 4 round beads using the bead roller. Place an oval bead onto the rubber stamp, fold the stamp over it or place the second duplicate stamp on top.

2 Press down gently to form a teardrop bead. Repeat this step with the remaining 6 beads, except each time stamp all four sides, leaving you with 6 rectangle beads. Stamp all six sides of the round beads to achieve cube beads.

3 Poke a hole in each bead with the cocktail stick, then bake as per the manufacturer's instructions. Allow to cool, then apply Sandstone paint over the bead.

4 Sand some of the paint away to reveal the texture. You may choose to lightly apply a bit of Burnt Umber paint, which just gives extra dimension to the bead.

ASSEMBLING

Cut a 7.5-cm (3-in.) piece of wire and create a loop at one end. String on a round spacer, flat spacer, clay bead, flat spacer and round spacer. Loop the opposite end and trim off any excess wire. Repeat for all beads. Attach each set of beads together with jump rings, alternating between the rectangle and the cube. Add the clasp to the ends of the necklace.

TIP
● *Unmounted rubber stamps work the best. If the stamp is not long enough to fold over, purchase two of the same stamp. This allows you to stamp both sides at the same time without distortion.*

MASAI PENDANT

Simulating bone is a great way to incorporate an organic element in your designs. The easiest way is to alternate layers of translucent and sand colour – the lines become more distinct after the clay is baked.

MATERIALS

Polymer clay: Classic Translucent, Sahara
Pasta machine
Rubber stamp
Clay texture wheel
Burnt Umber acrylic paint
400 grit sandpaper
61-cm (24-in.) length of leather cording
Tri-bead roller
Three eye pins
Two earring wires
Gloss varnish

Necklace

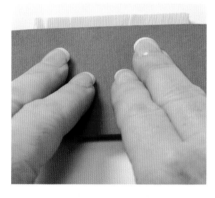

1 Flatten a sheet of each colour clay by passing through the pasta machine on medium thickness. Stack the sheets, then pass through the pasta machine to remove air bubbles. Create three more sets then stack all the sheets. Pass a sheet of Sahara through the machine on the thickest setting.

2 Slice thin sections off the bone stack and use to cover the Sahara sheet. Put this through the machine on the thickest setting then continue until you get to the third thinnest. Fold the stack in half, with the bone effect on the outside. Stamp a pattern into the sheet of clay.

3 Trim out a flat rectangle with a section of design. Trim an eye pin to 1 cm (½ in.) and press into the top centre of your focal pendant. Make smaller panels for the earrings. For the cylinder bead, use the texture wheel to create two lines 1 cm (½ in.) apart on the bone sheet.

4 Cut on the outside of the lines. Wrap around the end of a thick pencil or dowel, smoothing the seam. Twist a thin log of bone clay and wrap around each end.

ASSEMBLING

Bake the flat rectangle pieces and beads. Allow to cool, then apply Burnt Umber paint. Allow to dry, then sand the paint to reveal the pattern. Apply sealer if desired. Measure how long you want your necklace to be and add 15 cm (6 in.) to allow for knotting. Thread the cylinder bead to the centre of a length of leather cording. Loop the end around the bottom of the cylinder bead and back through the opposite side. Repeat this step with the other side. Knot the leather each side of the cylinder bead. String on a rectangle bead, knot, then three disks, knot.

Repeat for the other side. Open the loop at the top of your pendant and hang onto the leather cording. Add the large round bead to the end of the leather cord and knot in place. Make a loop big enough to go over this bead in the other end and knot.

Earrings

Open the loop at the top of the eye pin on an earring piece and slot on another eye pin. Add a round bead to this eye pin followed by a flattened spacer bead. Loop the other end of the eye pin with pliers and trim off excess wire. Attach earring wires.

IVORY COAST

MATERIALS

Polymer clay: Classic Translucent,
Sahara, cane decorations
Scrap clay
Oval focal bead roller
Head pin
Two bead caps
61-cm (24-in.) length of leather
cording
Toggle fastener

These beads are inspired by a well-known polymer clay artist, Karen Lewis, aka KLEW. Among my favourites are her 'drum' beads, which led to this necklace. Experiment by creating several sizes of base beads to embellish. This simple necklace will give you a jump start.

1 Make the striped clay as described in the Masai Pendant on page 42. Cut a thin sheet from the bone stripe stack and apply around a large oval base bead. When finished, lay the bead back into bead roller. Apply the top and gently roll smooth.

2 Create a variety of canes using the Caning techniques as described on pages 18–20. Decorate the focal bead by applying these slices, using the photographs as a guide.

TIP
● *When making the striped bone effect your lines do not have to be perfect – in fact some imperfections and irregularities add to the authenticity of the effect.*

3 Poke a hole through the focal bead and bake. Add a bead cap to a head pin, then thread on the bead.

ASSEMBLING
Thread another bead cap at the other end of the bead. Make a loop at the top of the head pin, then trim off the excess wire. Thread the bead onto a leather cord and attach your desired toggle fastener.

TURQUOISE ON CORD

Turquoise comes in a variety of forms, some beads are chunky and look like nuggets picked right up off the ground, others are smooth and refined. You will also find turquoise in a variety of colour combinations, some quite blue, others more green. This project is a way to create the look of turquoise in its simplest form.

MATERIALS

Polymer clay: Peppermint, Classic Translucent

Pro-bead roller set #1

Black acrylic paint

Round oval bead roller set (13 mm, 16 mm, 18 mm)

Alcohol-based ink: Rust, Ginger

Make-up sponges

Sealer (optional)

Approximately 183-cm (72-in.) length of black leather cording

Variety of silver spacer beads in different shapes and sizes

Two head pins

Two silver cone beads

Epoxy glue

Toggle fastener

1 Mix equal parts of Peppermint and Classic Translucent clay. Chop up some of this Turquoise mix, add a clump into the bead roller and gently press on the lid. Roll back and forth until the chunks are compressed together – you do not want smooth beads, rather some with small cracks and crevasses. Make a variety of beads: ovals, larger balls, flattened ovals etc.

TIP
● *To save time on future projects, you can create more mix than you will need at one time. This will give you extra clay ready to work with should you decide to come back at another time and create more beads or matching jewellery pieces.*

2 For some larger and rougher beads that will vary the look of your necklace and make it look more like the real thing, shape some of the chopped-up clay into rounded beads by hand.

3 Decide on the length of your necklace and add 30.5 cm (12 in.). Cut three cords to this length. Knot together 2.5 cm (1 in.) from one end. Working on separate cords, measure down 2.5 cm (1 in.) and knot, thread on bead, knot to hold in place.

ASSEMBLING

Repeat this technique on all strands, alternating turquoise beads with silver spacer beads. At times knot two cords together to keep all the strands together.

Thread a head pin into the cone bead and create a loop at the end. Trim off the leather cords and pin. together so that they will fit up inside the cone bead. Glue into place with epoxy glue – allow the glue to set thoroughly before wearing. Add the toggle fastener to the jump rings on the cone beads.

TURQUOISE NECKLACE

There are many ways to create turquoise. The vivid blue and green with black veining seen here is so dramatic, but it is made just like the marble on page 35. Again, a variation of colour makes the beads look more authentic.

Necklace

1 Shape a large focal bead in plain Black clay between the palms of your hands, pulling the top up into a rounded point with your fingertips. Make slices of turquoise effect in the same way as shown in the White Marble Necklace on page 35.

2 Add some slices of turquoise effect to the black focal bead and press in place. You are going for somewhat of a natural torn edge effect – do not cover the entire surface of the bead with turquoise marbled clay.

3 The necklace beads are also hand-formed and randomly shaped. Push an eye pin down into top centre of the focal bead. Shape a few into cubes. Poke holes through all beads and bake for one hour. Sand all beads beginning with 400 to 800 grit. This is a necessary step; it is okay to have slight cracks in the turquoise clay but you want the black areas to be smooth. Antique the surface with the Rust and Ginger inks, using a make-up sponge to dab on the colour.

TIP
● *Use a cocktail stick to draw the gold line as you can throw it away afterwards – you will need special oil based cleaners for a paintbrush.*

ASSEMBLING

Attach beading wire to a jump ring and string beads as follows: small spacer, large silver bead, small spacer, black accent bead, bead cap, turquoise bead. Continue with a bead cap on each side of the turquoise and a black bead between each pair. Attach a jump ring to the beading wire after the fifth set, add three round chain links joined with jump rings. Continue in beading sequence as before. Attach the focal pendant to the centre of the chain. Add the toggle fastener.

Earrings

Make up two triangular beads as for the necklace. Push a head pin through the centre, thread on a spacer bead, then form a loop on top and cut off the excess wire. Attach the beads to earring wires.

CHUNKY CORAL

Coral in this deep red colour is highly valued, but you can easily make your own. The cool tones of the silver beads used here really accentuate the fiery look of the coral. Try mixing coral with turquoise, amber or sterling silver – real coral does sometimes have different colour markings.

MATERIALS

Polymer clay: Classic Translucent, Indian Red, Mandarin Orange, Sunflower Yellow, Peppermint

Tube bead roller (7 mm, 9 mm)

Pasta machine

Heat gun

26-gauge craft wire

Rock with texture or coarse sandpaper

Burnt Umber acrylic paint

Sealer (optional)

Beading wire

Two jump rings

Two crimp beads

Two large silver spacers

Ten medium silver spacers

Twenty flat silver spacers

Toggle fastener

PREPARATION

Mix the coral colour using 3 parts Classic Translucent, 2 parts Indian Red, 1 part Mandarin Orange, and ¼ part Sunflower Yellow. To create a 40.5-cm (16-in.) choker necklace, create 4 beads with the 9 mm tube bead roller, 10 irregular rounded beads and one larger focal bead.

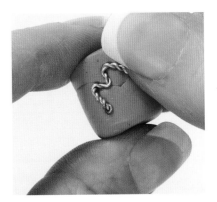

1 To create the turquoise insets, flatten a sheet of Peppermint on the second thinnest setting of the pasta machine. Heat the layer of clay with the heat gun to make it brittle.

2 Break off little pieces of the Peppermint sheet in random shapes. Push these small bits into one or two sides of some of the coral tube beads.

3 Twist a small piece of wire and shape into a 'W' and press into the side of the bead – this replicates the way antique coral is fixed when it naturally splits apart.

Press small texture marks into the bead with sandpaper or rock. Do not put too many, or when you antique the bead it will appear too dark. Bake all beads. Allow to cool and antique with Burnt Umber acrylic paint as described on page 22. Apply sealer if desired or buff on denim.

ASSEMBLING

Attach beading wire to a jump ring with a crimp bead, then thread beads onto the wire with the silver spacer beads between, following the sequence shown in the photograph. Finish by threading on a crimp bead. Loop the wire end over a jump ring, then thread the end back through the crimp bead, pull tight, then use crimping pliers to crimp. Attach the toggle fastener to each end of the necklace.

Variation: Choker

To create the choker necklace, create 28 beads with the 9 mm tube bead roller – add more beads for length, or to create a matching bracelet. Cut each bead about 1 cm (½ in.) long, but vary the width slightly. Thread the beads onto beading wire then attach a toggle or clasp to each end of the necklace.

CORAL TREE BRACELET

I love creating these coral branches, they remind me of tiny flickers of fire. By recreating the look of coral instead of using the real thing you are helping the environment, because coral is not a sustainable resource.

MATERIALS

Polymer clay: Classic Translucent, Indian Red, Mandarin Orange, Sunflower Yellow

Rock with texture or coarse sandpaper

Burnt Umber acrylic paint

Sealer (optional)

Beading wire

Two crimp beads

Three jump rings

Length of chain

Lobster clasp

TIP
● *You'll notice that on this bracelet I've added a chain, which is a nice way to make the bracelet adjustable to a variety of sizes. It's especially good if you are making pieces as a gift and do not know the person's correct size.*

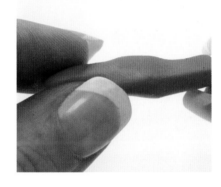

PREPARATION
Use the mix above to create the coral colour clay as described on page 50. With this technique you will make the branches in a variety of sizes, some small, some larger. For a 18-cm (7-in.) bracelet, you will need approximately 40 branches.

1 Make a small log in coral clay. Push and twist with your fingers to make it an uneven thickness along its length and to give the shape a few kinks like natural coral.

2 Add extra branches to some pieces of coral, smoothing the join with a clay shaper tool. Use the tip of the clay shaper to grab the clay and 'paint' away the seam.

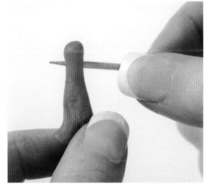

ASSEMBLING
Bake all the beads for 1 hour and allow to cool. Apply paint to antique, as described on page 22. Apply sealer if desired, or buff on denim. Cut a piece of beading wire 20 cm (8 in.) long and attach it to a jump ring with a crimp bead. String on the branches and finish with a crimp bead and jump ring. Add a short length of chain to one end of the bracelet with a jump ring, then add the lobster clasp.

3 Texture the surface of the coral beads, using a pumice stone or something similar such as a rock or coarse sandpaper.

4 Make a hole through one end of the length of coral, rather than through the centre each time, so it will hang from the bracelet.

CORAL WIRE BRACELET

This is a great project if you have a few leftover beads that you want to use.
I especially like this chunky wrapped look with coral, but it will look great
with other types of beads as well. The wire needs to be quite thick
or the beads will overpower it – but try the same idea with thinner wire
and finer beads for a very different look.

MATERIALS

Two coral tube beads
One hand-formed bead
14-gauge silver wire
Selection of various silver beads
Selection of various silver spacers
Selection of various silver bead caps

TIPS

● *When you are wrapping the wire,
don't cut it off the spool at the start
– just pull out a length to work with
and only cut it off when you come to
attach the end. That way you are not
limited as to how much wire you
have to work with.*

● *You can adjust the length of the
clasp by coiling the spiral of the hook
a little more.*

1 Measure your wrist and add
2.5 cm (1 in.). Cut a length of
wire to this measurement and create
a loop in one end. Thread on some
silver and coral beads, using the
photograph as a guide. At the end,
make another loop in the wire to
hold everything in place.

2 Generally I work off the spool, so
I am sure I have enough wire for
what I want to do. Attach the end of
the wire by twisting it around the
end of the bracelet several times.
Loop the wire around the entire
bracelet randomly, to create an
interesting pattern.

3 Finish by wrapping the wire
around the last bead. Cut another
piece of wire 10 cm (4 in.) long.
Coil one end, then bend the other
end upward and double back. Turn
this end back into a decorative coil.

4 Bend over the doubled end of
the wire to make a fastening
hook. Open the loop at one end of
the bracelet and place the spiral end
onto it. Close the hook. The hook
will attach into the other loop.

CORAL DROPS ENSEMBLE

The hanging glass drops on this necklace look just like little drops of water glinting in the sunlight and they swing free to add movement to the whole design. The large gold links used here are just a chain taken apart – don't be afraid to use findings in different ways.

MATERIALS

Polymer clay: Classic Translucent
Tri-bead roller
Alcohol-based inks: Rust, Ginger or colours of choice
Make-up sponge
Spray bottle with isopropyl alcohol
Sixteen eye pins
Thirteen large oval gold chain links
Twenty-eight gold jump rings
Eight glass drops
24-gauge silver non-tarnish wire
26-gauge copper wire
Cocktail sticks
Toggle fastener
Two earring wires

Necklace

1 Create 16 puff beads using the tri-bead roller as described on page 14. Poke a hole through each bead and bake. Place the white bead on a cocktail stick and dab coral-coloured alcohol ink across the surface with a make-up sponge.

page 14.

TIPS

● *You can continue to apply more ink to the bead to achieve a more contrasting effect.*

● *Too much alcohol will cause the ink to run and smear. You just want light droplets to hit the clay to achieve this effect. If you are unsatisfied with the results, spray the entire bead with alcohol, rub off with a wipe and begin again.*

● *Hanging the crystal from the jump ring connecting the links stops it falling to the base of the large link when the necklace is worn. There are two links that do not have droplets. This marks the top of the necklace so that the droplets will all fall in the right direction.*

2 Spray gently across the entire surface of the bead with isopropyl alcohol to achieve the watermarked colour effect.

3 Add a jump ring to one of the large chain links. Add another jump ring to the crystal drop, then hang this from the first jump ring.

ASSEMBLING

Thread an eye pin through a bead, and bend the other end round into a loop to match the eye. Repeat on all the beads. Use the photograph as a guide to make up the necklace, with alternate beads and links, connected with jump rings. The links with the hanging crystals come at the front of the necklace. Add the toggle fastener.

Earrings

Make up the earrings by attaching earring wires to the last two beads.

BLUE HAWAII NECKLACE

The Hawaiian islands have a wonderful tradition of presenting you with a *lei*, or garland of flowers, when you arrive. Fresh flowers soon fade and die, but this exotic pewter bloom on its garland of green and blue stones will last forever! The necklace is 46 cm (18 in.) long – adjust amount of beads for larger sizes.

MATERIALS

Polymer clay: Metallic White
Tube bead roller set #2
Piercing pins
Alcohol-based ink: Lime Green, Baja Blue, Sapphire Blue
Make-up sponge
Spray bottle with isopropyl alcohol (optional)
Beading wire
Four jump rings
Four crimp beads
Twenty-four 3 mm roundel silver spacer beads
Four 3 mm round spacer beads
Twelve 3 mm spacer beads with pattern
Thin cardstock
Double-sided tape
1 sheet pewter metal
Wooden stylus
Clay texture wheel
Three 6 mm green faceted glass beads
Toggle fastener
Quick-set epoxy glue

PREPARATION

Following the directions on the tube bead roller, create approximately one-hundred and fifty 6 mm tube beads. These can be rolled by hand if you do not have a tube bead roller. Cut into 5-mm (¼-in.) sections and place on piercing pins to bake according to the manufacturer's instructions.

1 Daub Lime Green ink onto 32 tube beads, Baja Blue onto 88 beads and the remainder with Sapphire Blue. If you want an irregular pattern to the beads, lightly spray with isopropyl alcohol to create the watermarked effect. Attach two lengths of beading wire to jump rings with crimp beads. Both strands are identical – use the photo as your guide for stringing. Secure the end of the wire with crimp beads and repeat the combination for second strand.

2 Trace the flower template on page 126 onto cardstock and cut out. Apply double-sided tape to one side, then remove the backing to reveal the adhesive.

3 Place the card template adhesive side down onto a sheet of pewter metal. Cut out the flower shape in the pewter, leaving an extra 2.5-mm (⅛-in.) wide border around all the edges. The pewter is very soft so you will be able to cut it with ordinary scissors.

4 Using the wooden stylus, fold the edges of the metal right over the edge of the cardstock shape and flatten on the reverse side. Apply double-sided tape over the reverse of the flower shape, then expose the adhesive as before.

TIP
● Make sure the cylinder is big enough for the beads to thread through. If not, wrap it around the beads before gluing it to the back of the flower.

5 Place the flower adhesive-side down onto the pewter and cut out, this time leaving no extra border. Smooth the edges with the wooden stylus.

6 Repeat Steps 2–5 again to make a second flower shape. Emboss a design on the front of all of the petals with the stylus and clay texture tool, using the photograph on page 60 as a guide.

7 Punch holes as marked on the template and thread wire through both petal sets. Glue glass beads to the centre of the flower.

8 Shape the petals of the flower into an attractive curve.

9 Cut a strip of pewter 2.5 cm (1 in.) wide by 7.5 cm (3 in.) long. Fold the edges to the centre and flatten them with the stylus.

10 Wrap the strip of pewter around a finger to create a cylinder. Tape to hold the join in place and trim any excess metal.

11 Glue the cylinder onto the back of the flower. Allow the glue to set thoroughly overnight, then string beads through the loop.

ART DECO SET

The wonderfully decadent art deco shapes and colours of this necklace and earrings give them an authentic period look, even though the materials used are so modern. Foiled clay is so easy to work with when wrapping 3-D shapes – much more so than trying to use the very thin sheets of foil alone.

MATERIALS

Polymer clay: Black
Pasta machine
Metallic foils: Gold, Pink, Silver, Blue, Purple
Three flat backed Swarovski crystals
Ultra-thick embossing enamel (UTEE)
Melting pot
Heat gun
Cocktail stick
24-gauge silver wire
Six bi-cone Swarovski crystals
Round-nose pliers
Silver chain
Toggle fastener
Two earring wires
Three jump rings

Necklace and earrings

1 Roll a sheet of Black clay to the second thinnest setting on the pasta machine. Place the foil sheet, colour side up, onto the clay and rub it briskly. The friction of your fingers creates heat, which will allow the foil to adhere to the clay.

2 Rip the backing off the foil quickly. Small areas of the foil may not fully transfer and that is okay. Repeat for each colour.

3 Flatten some Black clay on the thickest setting and double. Using the template on page 126, cut out the base shape from the clay.

4 Wrap the foiled clay over the base shape. Add an additional colour so that the shape is two-toned. Trim off any excess.

5 Cut a wedge shape from contrasting foiled clay. Bend the narrow point into sinuous curves to make an interesting shape.

6 Add a large and small circle to fill in as desired. You can press a crystal into the circle to give it extra bling. Make a hole through the centre of the bead, then bake.

7 Heat up the UTEE until it melts. Thread the baked bead onto a cocktail stick through the centre hole and plug the other end of the hole with a chopped off cocktail stick to seal it temporarily. Dip the bead into the molten UTEE.

8 Remove the bead from the UTEE, but hold it up above the melting pot for a minute or so – this will allow the excess UTEE to run back into the pot.

9 Cut around the base of the cocktail stick at each end of the bead. This will help to release the bead easily and cleanly from the cocktail stick.

TIPS

● *You can store leftover foiled clay between layers of clingfilm for future use.*

● *Start making the hole from the point of the triangle and work downwards – if you work the other way, the hole may not come out on the very point.*

10 Pull the cocktail stick plug out gently from the bottom end of the bead.

11 Use a heat gun to melt the UTEE slightly to round off around the end of the bead nicely.

12 Cut a 10-cm (4-in.) length of wire. Make a circular eye at one end then thread on a crystal bi-cone bead, bead shape then another crystal bi-cone bead. Using the round-nose pliers, curl the other end of the wire around into an attractive spiral.

13 Attach the finished beads to the earring wires or the chain with jump rings.

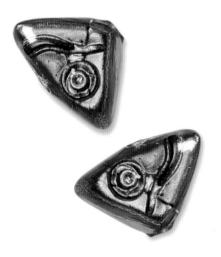

TIPS

● *If you are working in a cool workplace, the top layer of the UTEE may be a little thicker than desired even though the melting pot is set to the right temperature. If this is the case, heat across the UTEE with a heat gun and it will quickly become more liquefied.*

● *The Ultra-thick embossing enamel (UTEE) is runny when hot and hard when cold, so if you have a drip, or a finger mark, or the enamel is just too thick, heat the area up with a heat gun and the UTEE will go runny again and smooth out.*

NEW YORK DISCO BALLS

The vibrant city of New York, with its bright lights and vivid colours, inspired these glowing metallic orbs. They rather remind me of the mirror balls that used to be common in dance halls! Again, the metallic foil is applied to a thin sheet of clay and then used to cover a base ball in scrap clay.

MATERIALS
Polymer clay: Black
Pasta machine
Metallic foils: Pink, Orange
Scrap clay
Large round bead roller (optional)
Forty-four Swarovski crystals – flat backed and bi-cone
24-gauge silver wire
Ultra-thick embossing enamel (UTEE)
Melting pot
Heat gun
Two spacer beads
Circle clay cutters: 5 and 2.5 mm (¼ and ⅛ in.)
Crinkle beading wire
Twenty-four crimp beads
Two jump rings
Toggle fastener

PREPARATION
Make up the metallic foiled clay as described on page 63, with half of it pink and half orange. Make 11 round base beads in scrap clay, using the bead roller or by hand.

1 Cover half of base beads with pink foil covered clay and the other half with orange foil covered clay. Shape gently into the ends, and then shape the bead into a ball, or re-shape with the bead roller. Cut several circles from orange and pink foiled clay using the 5-mm (¼-in.) and 2.5-mm (⅛-in.) cutters.

2 On the orange ball beads, apply a 5-mm (¼-in.) pink with a 2.5-mm (⅛-in.) orange in the centre. Push a crystal into the centre of 4 orange circles. Reverse colouring on the pink beads. There are six bull's-eye embellishments on the bead. Poke the threading hole through the centre of the small circles that do not have the crystals.

3 Bake the beads, then dip into melted Ultra-thick embossing enamel (UTEE). Clean any mistakes with a heat gun.

ASSEMBLING
Thread the beads alternately onto the lengths of wire, with crimp beads on each side to hold them in position approximately 4 cm (1½ in.) apart.

KYOTO PENDANT

Adding images to your clay is a great way to include more detail and to create a wonderful period look in your jewellery pieces. There are a lot of ways to transfer images, but I've chosen the simplest and the most foolproof, the water slide technique. It works well with these projects and you will get great results nearly every time.

MATERIALS

Polymer clay: Black
Scrap clay
Asian image
Water slide transfer paper
Spray bottle with water
Gloss varnish
61-cm (24-in.) length of leather cording
Bead
Epoxy glue (optional)

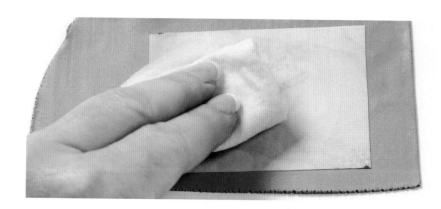

PREPARATION

Create a flattened cylindrical base bead in scrap clay the same length as the height of your transfer and approximately 1 cm (½ in.) in diameter, using the photograph as a rough guide to shape. Bake the bead and allow to cool.

1 Roll out a flat sheet of pale colour clay to the medium setting on the pasta machine. Copy your chosen image onto the water slide transfer paper, using an ink-jet printer. Apply the transfer image side down to the sheet of clay and burnish with your fingers to remove any air pockets. Spray the back of the transfer with water. Wait approximately 30 seconds.

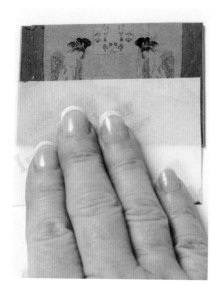

TIP
● It may be necessary to gently remove the ball at the top after baking and attach it with epoxy glue to ensure it has a strong bond.

2 Slide off the backing sheet. Cut out around the transfer and apply it around the baked bead, matching seams and trimming as necessary. Allow to dry, then paint the image with gloss varnish to protect it.

3 Flatten two balls of plain Black clay into disks and apply to top and bottom of the cylinder. Roll a small decorative ball to top each end. Poke a hole horizontally through the top ball. Bake the bead.

ASSEMBLING

Thread the focal bead onto the length of leather cording. Add the other bead to one end, thread the cord through again and knot the bead in place. Make a loop at the other end large enough to go over the bead and knot to secure.

MATERIALS

Polymer clay: Classic Translucent, Black, Cinnabar mix
Pasta machine
Asian image
Water slide transfer paper
Spray bottle with water
Rubber stamp for texture
Polyblade
Black acrylic paint
Gold leafing pen
Gloss varnish
61-cm (24-in.) length of leather cording
Toggle fastener

JAPANESE PENDANT

I found this image of a Japanese lady in traditional costume and decided to make a pendant with a Japanese look. This project is a good one to learn water slide techniques to transfer images to clay.

PREPARATION

Size and print your desired image onto the water slide transfer paper using an ink-jet printer. Cut out the image and trim to size. Flatten the Translucent sheet of clay on the thickest setting of the pasta machine. Apply the transfer as described on page 69. Bake the tile for 30 minutes.

1 Flatten Black clay on the thickest setting of the pasta machine, then position the transfer tile on the centre of the sheet. Flatten Cinnabar clay (see page 29 for Cinnabar mix) on the thickest setting. Apply a texture design with a rubber stamp and cut out strips to frame the transferred image.

2 Trim off the excess Black from around the frame. Notice that I have bent my polyblade to make the curved shape at the top. The sides are angled.

TIP
● *When I want the image to wrap a bead I use a photo-editing program, reverse the image and paste it next to the original. Save this file as a new image. Then the final image is long enough to go around the entire bead without having to piece it together.*

3 Roll out four logs approximately 5 mm (¼ in.) in diameter in Black clay and frame the pendant again. Cut out the pendant shape leaving a small border in Black – this finishes off the edges and makes them look smooth.

4 Flatten small balls for the top and bottom of the pendant. Create a loop for the leather cord with a small log – taper both ends and press one end on the front and one on the back. Cover the front join with a flattened ball. Bake again for 1 hour.

ASSEMBLING
Apply black paint to the Cinnabar textured surface and sand smooth to reveal the pattern. Add a gold line to frame the picture. Apply gloss varnish to protect everything. Thread the pendant onto the leather cord and apply the toggle fastener.

MEMORY BRACELET

This bracelet includes photos of a recent holiday – you can print pictures of your family, your favourite things, whatever you like. Add themed charms and you have a charming aide-memoir! This is another transfer technique using dark T-shirt transfer, which is rubbery. It is set with heat and so bonds to the clay after baking.

MATERIALS

Polymer clay: White or other light colour
Pasta machine
Dark T-shirt transfer paper
Photos sized down to thumbnail size
Eye pins, one for each tile
5-mm (¼-in.) double-sided tape
Pewter metal sheet
Wooden stylus
Liquid polymer gel
Embossing heat gun
Epoxy glue
Gloss varnish
Pre-made bracelet chain
Jump rings, one for each tile
Silver charms of choice

PREPARATION

Flatten the clay on the thickest setting of the pasta machine. Fold over the sheet to create a double thickness. Copy the photos onto the transfer paper and then cut them out, without a border.

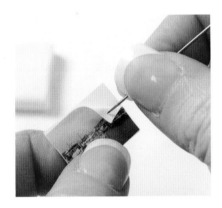

1 Carefully peel the backing off the image and apply it to the clay. Burnish gently to make sure that there are no air bubbles. Trim the clay tile exactly to the size of the image. Trim an eye pin down to 1 cm (½ in.) and press into the top centre of each tile. Bake the tiles and then remove the eye pins.

TIP
● *Print multiple pictures, in case one gets ruined during the tile making process. Or make several tiles for additional bracelets.*

● *The gel goes from translucent, to milky, to clear when heated. Until it is completely clear it is not set.*

2 After baking, apply double-sided tape around the edges of the tile. Cut a strip of pewter 5-mm (¼-in.) wide. Remove the backing on the double-sided tape and wrap the pewter around the edges of the tile, beginning at the hole in the top, and leaving just a hairline of the pewter sticking above the tile front. Press the edges down over the tile with a wooden stylus on both front and back. Apply double-sided tape to the back of the tile. Remove the tape backing and place the tile onto the pewter. Cut out flush and use the stylus to soften the edges of the tile. Add a semi-thick layer of liquid polymer gel to the surface of the tile to give it a glass-like look.

3 Heat the liquid polymer gel with a heat gun to set it. Constantly rotate the heat gun to keep the gel from forming a depression in the middle and don't get the heat gun too close as the air from it will push the gel over the sides. I generally heat at an angle and rotate to set each edge first, then heat the top.

ASSEMBLING

Apply gloss varnish to all the tiles. Replace the eye pins and glue in place. Attach the tiles to the bracelet with jump rings and add themed charms.

MATERIALS

Polymer clay: Black

Pasta machine

Peel-off metallic (outline) stickers, at least two of same design

Liquid polymer gel

Mica powders in colours of choice

Cocktail sticks

Embossing heat gun

Gloss varnish

Eye pin

61-cm (24-in.) length of leather cording and toggle fastener

CLOISONNÉ FLOWER

This jazzy flower is a dramatic piece to wear when you are feeling like the star of the show! Outline stickers are ideal to use when you want to define the edges of different colours in a design – just like in cloisonné enamel or stained glass. And the lines of the design can be far more detailed than you can draw.

1 Flatten Black clay on the thickest setting and cut out a shape – use the template on page 126 or make your own. Make a hole with an eye pin at the top, then bake the shape and allow to cool. Remove the eye pin, choose a sticker and apply to baked shape. You can place it off-centre for an interesting look, just trim off any excess.

2 Mix a selection of mica powder colours into little pools of the liquid polymer gel. Use a separate cocktail stick to mix each colour and to 'paint' the colours with – this will save having to clean up brushes at the end as the cocktail sticks can just be thrown away.

ASSEMBLING

Apply the same sticker in the same position on the pendant, right over the top of the existing one – this will fix any minor outline mistakes. Apply a thin layer of gel over the top and bake. After cooling, apply gloss sealer. Add the eye pin to the top and glue in place with epoxy adhesive. Attach the pendant to the cording.

3 Paint the colours into the spaces between the lines, blending colours like real enamelling. Don't be concerned too much with staying in the lines since this will be fixed later. However, you don't want so much gel that it totally bleeds over the outlines.

4 Set the gel with the heat gun. Apply a thin clear coat of gel over the entire top, then bake in the oven. Apply another thin clear coat of gel over the entire top, bake in the oven again and then finish off with the heat gun.

TIP
● *Work on a ceramic tile and for an easy clean up, set any spilt gel with a heat gun or bake in the oven. After cooling, peel the gel right off!*

CHAPTER 2

Mokume' Gane' Technique

Mokume' Gane' is an ancient Japanese way of working that has been adapted for use with polymer clay. The pattern comes by creating many thin layers of coloured clay, impressing a texture into the layers and then shaving thin slices away to reveal the design. There are so many ways to work this technique and so many possible outcomes, that the results are never boring. This chapter highlights a couple of simple ways to achieve this effect, including using different colour clays, colouring with alcohol inks and different things you can impress into the clay. Experiment with this technique; there is no wrong way to do it. Remember, there are no mistakes, only happy accidents… so enjoy the journey!

GOLD AND STONE FOCAL BEAD

This unusual necklace has a wonderfully rich focal bead, wrapped with golden wire and hung from a leather cord. With this Mokume' Gane' technique, the colour comes from the use of alcohol inks. These inks are transparent so you can alter their intensity by adding more ink, or you can daub some away for a more subtle effect.

MATERIALS

Polymer clay: Classic Translucent
Pasta machine
Easy metal: Silver or Gold leaf
Alcohol-based ink: colours of choice
Make-up sponge
Roller (optional)
Rubber stamp or texture of choice
Polyblade
Base bead
Thin gold-coloured wire
61-cm (24-in.) length of leather cording or purchased chain
Clasp or other fastener

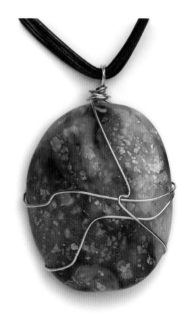

1 Flatten the Classic Translucent clay on the thinnest setting of the pasta machine. Cut into several sheets, then add silver or gold leaf to the top of a sheet of clay.

2 Apply alcohol ink over the top of the metal leaf sheet with a make-up sponge. Colours will mix as they come together, creating new colours.

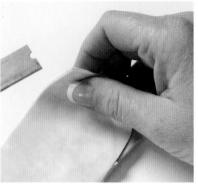

3 Add another thin sheet of Classic Translucent clay over the top of your metal leaf sheet and smooth into position.

4 Cut the layered clay into four sections and stack these one on top of the other to create lots more alternate layers.

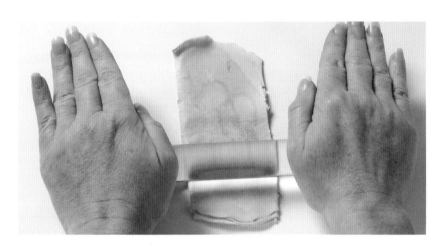

5 Roll out the clay with a roller, removing any air bubbles and elongating the stack – you can also do this through the pasta machine. Cut in half and stack. You should be noticing that the layers are getting thinner, but the colour is not mixing.

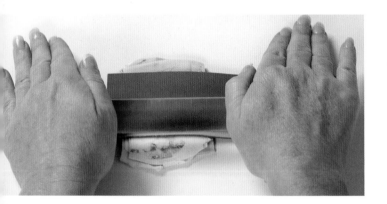

6 Impress a pattern into the clay, making sure you create a deep impression. The pattern itself is not at all important, you only want to use it to create a marble of different colours across the area.

7 With the polyblade bent, cut paper-thin pieces from the top of the clay and set aside. Notice that only a small portion of my blade is actually shaving the pattern. It is better to go over a section again, than to take one deep slice.

9 Bake the bead. When it is cool, wrap the finished bead in wire, creating a loop at the top as you work on which to hang the bead.

8 Apply some of the shavings to a plain base bead. This base bead can be any co-ordinating colour – for the photographs we have used a translucent one, in order to make the lovely colours in the shaved layers pop out even more.

ASSEMBLING
Hang the finished pendant from a length of leather cord and add a clasp or fastener of your choice, or hang it from a finished chain.

BLUES BRACELET

I purchased a bracelet while on a business trip – it was sort of a present to myself. After studying it further, I realised I could duplicate the look of stones set in sterling silver by using pewter, which is much softer and easier to work. This bracelet is an adaptation of the purchased one.

MATERIALS

Polymer clay: Brilliant Blue, White, Classic Translucent
Pasta machine
Easy metal: Gold or Silver leaf
Found objects for creating texture and interesting patterns
Rectangular base beads with rounded edges
Double-sided tape, 5-mm (¼-in.) and 2.5-cm (1-in.)
Pewter metal sheet
Wooden stylus
24-gauge non-tarnish silver wire
Round-nose pliers
Scissors
Twelve jump rings
Toggle fastener or clasp

PREPARATION

With this style of Mokume' Gane', the colour comes from different colours of clay. You will need to select your base colour – in this project we used Brilliant Blue. Use White to make light and medium blue so you have three different tints to work with. Roll out all colours to the thinnest setting on the pasta machine. Stack in the following order: Brilliant Blue, Translucent, metal leaf, medium, Translucent, metal leaf, light, Translucent. Flatten the stack through the pasta machine on the thickest setting, or roll by hand. Cut and stack just as you did in the Gold and Stone Focal Bead project on page 80.

1 Notice some of the things that you can use to create an interesting pattern. They include a stylus, for making dots, bone folder for making lines and circle cutter for making circles. Impress these into the clay in a pleasing design. Cut shavings as before to reveal a pattern. Place shavings onto base beads. Bake the beads and allow to cool.

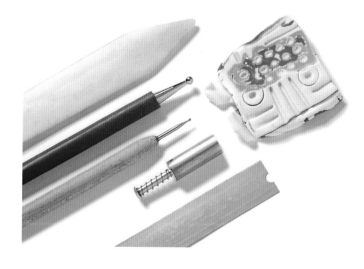

2 Using the 5-mm (¼-in.) wide double-sided tape, wrap a thin strip of tape around the edge of the baked bead. Take off the tape backing.

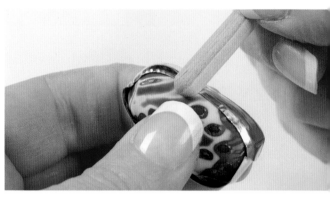

3 Cut the pewter sheet into 5-mm (¼-in.) wide strips. Wrap a strip of pewter around the stone right on top of the double-sided tape.

4 Lay the edges of the metal over the front of the stone with a wooden stylus. The pewter is soft and will contour easily to the shape of the stone.

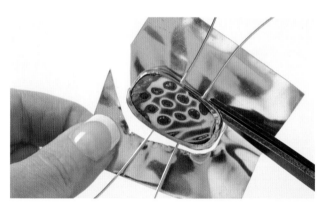

5 Apply double-sided tape to the back of the stone and remove the backing. Put two 10-cm (4-in.) long lengths of silver wire across the back, fixed in place on the tape. Apply more tape over wire and remove the backing.

6 Place a layer of pewter on the back, right over the wires. Trim it flush all around the side of the stone, using the scissors. Be careful not to snip the wires – you may not cut through but you could damage them.

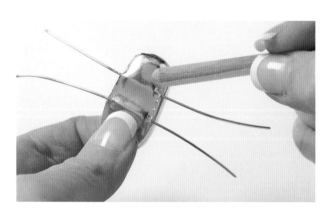

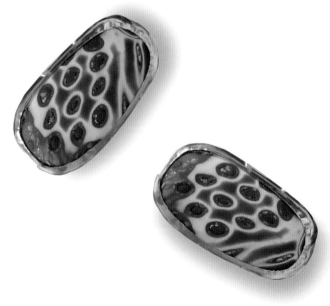

7 Burnish the backing sheet around the edges to join it to the side strip of pewter.

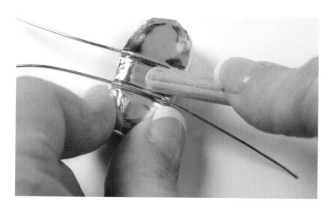

8 Burnish down carefully between the wires at the back to make sure that the metal is joined all around with no gaps.

9 Using round-nose pliers, bend the wires around to form the loops on each side of the stone. Cut off excess wire.

ASSEMBLING

Attach the stones together using the jump rings. Add a toggle fastener or a clasp at each end.

Variation: Blue Stone Necklace

This bracelet is quite heavy and chunky, so if you would like to make a co-ordinating necklace it is better to make a short length of beads and add a length of chain, rather than just making an extra-long bracelet.

To create a necklace, make up hree or four beads as desired, as described in Steps 1–9. Join these together in a row in the same way as for the bracelet. Attach a matching length of chain on each side of the row of beads, then add the fastener of your choice to the other end of the chain. This will give a much lighter necklace, but with the same look as your bracelet.

You can also use this pewter mounting technique on any of the simulated stone beads described on pages 26–75, to get the effect of expensive semi-precious jewellery at just a fraction of the cost!

SNAKESKIN LARIAT

The inspiration for this necklace came from an advert in a clothing magazine featuring gorgeous turquoise jewellery and a snakeskin coat. I knew I wanted to replicate the pattern in the coat and felt a measure of success when I succeeded. With this piece, I've used a piece of wire mesh to impress the pattern.

MATERIALS

Polymer clay: Plum, Black, Sahara, Classic Translucent
Pasta machine
Easy metal: Gold or Silver leaf
Small sheet of wire mesh
Roller
Polyblade
Approximately ten oval and round base beads
Gloss varnish
Seed bead mix
Approximately fourteen round black beads
Approximately six small crystal beads
Beading wire
Two crimp beads
Two jump rings
Two head pins

PREPARATION

Flatten all the colours of clay to the thinnest setting on the pasta machine. Stack in the following order: Plum, Translucent, metal leaf, Black, Translucent, metal leaf, Sahara, Translucent, metal leaf. Cut and stack as you did in the previous projects.

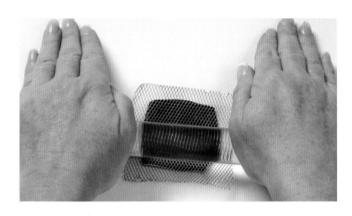

1 Press the wire mesh into the top of the layer of clay firmly with the roller.

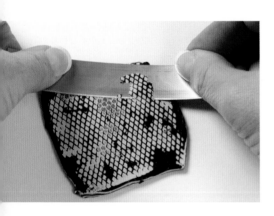

2 Shave off some layers. If you don't get a pattern or colours you like, press the mesh into the clay again and shave at a lower level until you get the desired effect that you want for your project.

3 Start pressing the patterned shavings onto the base bead. This particular bead had some leaf shavings on it that only add to the effect. Poke holes through the beads and bake. Sand smooth and apply gloss varnish.

ASSEMBLING

Lariat necklaces are one very long string, worn wrapped in strands around your neck, or just tied in the centre. Cut beading wire to length. Attach a jump ring to one end and thread seed beads randomly intermixed with snakeskin beads. Finish with a jump ring. Create two bead dangles with seed beads and snakeskin beads on head pins. Loop the top of the head pin and attach one to each end of the lariat.

> *TIP*
> ● *When you first shave, you get lots of tiny squares but the pattern reveals the more you shave. When you run out of pattern, impress the wire mesh again and again for different looks.*

CHAPTER 3

Sculpted Beads

This technique really combines my love of sculpting whimsical, happy characters with my love of jewellery and beads. Much of my inspiration comes from an artist named Christi Friesen – her whimsical designs are beautifully showcased in the art jewellery she creates. She was kind enough to let me share my version of her style with you. If you think you cannot sculpt shapes, just go back and refer to the Six Simple Shape™ technique on page 21 as this will greatly help you when sculpting. All of the shapes I use in the projects for this chapter utilise that technique. Just try it out – I promise it will work and before you know it you will be creating amazingly realistic forms.

SEA STRINGS

The fantastic fibres you can find these days are a great inspiration for jewellery items. These shown here reminded me of seaweed and so I created this under-the-sea necklace, with its turtle focal bead and starfish peeping out from amongst the threads. All the shapes are really simple, so get modelling!

MATERIALS

Polymer clay: Classic Translucent, Sahara, Peppermint, Black, Tropical Green, Lime Green, Emerald Green, Copper, Gold

Round ball stylus with small tip

Black and Burnt Umber acrylic paint

Paintbrush

Pasta machine

Circle pattern and circle punch

Two seed beads

Gold leafing pen

At least six different co-ordinating fibres

Quilting thread in a matching colour

Miscellaneous purchased shell beads (optional)

PREPARATION

You may also choose to interweave seed beads and other shell beads at various intervals on your necklace – if so, collect everything together before you begin so you can work around what you have available. I strung thread through the starfish I made and tied them onto the fibres of the necklace, but you may thread your starfish onto one of the main fibres instead.

1 To make the starfish, roll 1-cm (½-in.) ball of Sahara clay and flatten in slightly. Start to pull out five 'legs' around the edge to shape into a star. Refine the star shape.

TIP

● *I'm giving you sizes so that if you want to be precise you can. However, my saying is: 'If it looks too big, it is. Take away some clay. And if it looks too small, it is. Add some clay.'*

2 Use the clay shaper to get into the corners of the starfish. Real starfish are not perfect, so it doesn't matter if the legs are not all the same size and shape. Texture the surface of the starfish with the ball tipped stylus. Repeat for as many starfish as you wish in your necklace – I have used three. Bake the starfish, following the clay manufacturer's instructions.

3 To create a starfish that is textured on both sides, you will repeat the above steps, this time sculpting on the back of the already baked starfish. Poke a hole through the tip down through the bottom of the starfish. Gently rotate the cocktail stick making sure it isn't stuck to the clay. Bake. Apply brown paint and antique both sides of the starfish to bring out the highlights.

4 Flatten Black clay to the thickest setting on the pasta machine. Stack two sheets to make a double layer. Using a small round tin or circle pattern, cut out a circle to desired size. Use a circle punch to cut out the centre.

5 Round all the edges of the disk off with the tips of your fingers, both inside and out. You can decorate the disk with any stone effect from pages 26–75; here I am planning to use some turquoise (see page 46). Trim an eye pin down to around 5-mm (¼-in.) in length and stick it into the top of the disk so you will have something for the necklace strands to be attached to when you make your necklace up.

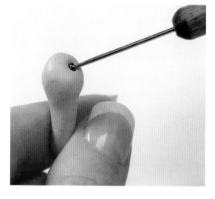

6 Start modelling the turtle. Shape a 1.5-cm (⅝-in.) ball of Sahara into a tapered log, rounding the end into a ball and then pinching the tip to make the face.

7 Add two black seed beads, placing them symmetrically on either side of the head for the eyes. Use the modelling tool to place the beads for accuracy.

8 Flatten a 5-mm (¼-in.) ball of Sahara and shape into a teardrop. Bend the teardrop shape around at the end. Make two little lines with a needle tool to finish the flipper. Repeat to make a total of four.

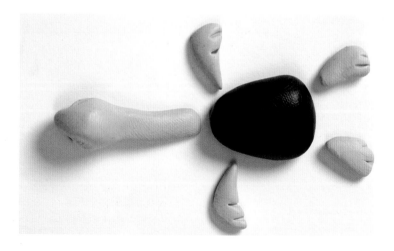

9 Use an oval in Black for the body shell. Here are the pieces laid out in position. Assemble the turtle, by placing the shell over the neck and flippers.

10 Roll out some tiny balls in a green colour, flatten them and apply around the base of the shell to decorate it. Add some detail to the shell with the modelling tool.

11 Marble some of the green colours together. Flatten and shape various sized marble balls into teardrops. Draw in veins on the leaf with a needle tool. Twist the leaf to give it some shape.

12 Place the turtle on the disk and add the leaves around, referring to the photograph of the finished necklace on page 91 as a guide. The seaweed is three shapes of copper twisted together into a rope and rolled small. Add some texture with the modelling tool and gold highlights with the leafing pen.

13 Cut six strands of different textured threads to your desired necklace length plus 15 cm (6 in.). Knot together in the centre, attaching the focal piece at the knot. Tie a loop on one side of the necklace and plait loosely, then knot the other end. Attach a starfish to the knot and thread a starfish through the opposite side loop to make the fastening.

GIRAFFE SAFARI

This cute little giraffe peering out from between lush tropical leaves is a great favourite whenever I do a show! You don't have to make a giraffe though – you can make any animal that you care to just by combining the basic shapes in different ways. Study photographs of real animals to give you some ideas.

MATERIALS

Polymer clay: Sahara, Black, Tropical Green, Lime Green, Emerald Green, Copper, Gold

Eye pin

Round ball stylus with small tip

Grey acrylic paint

Paintbrush

Pasta machine

Two black seed beads

Short length of wire

61-cm (24-in.) length of leather cording

Small bead

PREPARATION

We are using many of the same basic colours and materials here as in the Sea Strings project. Create a black marble bead using the marble technique on page 35, with Black clay and Grey paint. Add an eye pin at the top, then bake and sand it so it is ready to be embellished with the giraffe. For the completed project, I worked directly on the bead.

> ### TIP
> ● *Working on a tile will allow you to move the giraffe and work on it in various directions without touching it. The tile can then go directly into the oven.*

1 Using Sahara clay, create the following: 1-cm (½-in.) ball shaped into a teardrop (body); a 1.5-cm (⅝-in.) ball shaped into a teardrop; 5-mm (¼-in.) ball flattened. Here are the main pieces for the giraffe's body laid out so that you can see the refined shapes.

2 Add the head to the neck and blend the seam between the two with the clay shaper to get a smooth, continuous shape. Press a seed bead eye into the head, using the needle modelling tool.

3 Flatten small brown balls and add them for the spots. Texture slightly with the needle tool. Twist the ear into a curved shape and add to the giraffe, then add the mane, which is a roll of clay with texture added. Add leaves (see page 123 for instructions). For the stamen, thread 15 or so seed beads onto a piece of wire and attach at the base of the leaf. Add texture as required.

ASSEMBLING

Thread the pendant onto a doubled length of the leather cording. Knot a bead at one end and create a loop at the other to fasten over it.

SEAHORSE PENDANT

Seahorses are fascinating animals – the curvy shapes and shades of green and blue used here create an unusual and eye-catching pendant. Again, we are using the same basic modelling materials as in the Sea Strings project. I have also used a turquoise acrylic paint with a daub of gold metallic Rub-N-Buff.

MATERIALS

Polymer clay: Sahara
Round ball stylus with small tip
Two black seed beads
Eye pin
Turquoise acrylic paint
Paintbrush
Gold metallic Rub-N-Buff
Beading wire
Four jump rings
Four crimp beads
Large selection of seed beads in
metallic greens
Toggle fastener or clasp

1 The seahorse body is similar to the giraffe. Start with the same size and basic body shape. Elongate the body at both ends. Elongate at the lower end even further – this part will curl up for the tail. In this picture you see the various stages of shape. The head is exactly the same shape as the giraffe, except the nose is a little more blunt.

2 The component parts for the seahorse. The head has an elongated nose with a flattened snout. The tail is curled up. Create little spirals from small logs. Assemble the parts. Press seed bead eyes in with the needle tool.

3 Add additional texture and design to the seahorse as desired. You can see that I also flattened some balls and applied to his back for scales. This is where you can get very creative so that each seahorse has a personality of its own.

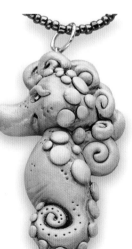

FINISHING

Press in an eye pin to the top of the seahorse and bake. Leave to cool. Antique the seahorse with turquoise acrylic paint. I also rubbed gold Rub-N-Buff on some areas to highlight and give it a gold cast.

ASSEMBLING

Add a jump ring to the end of a length of beading wire, securing with a crimp bead, and thread on half the seed beads. Finish with another jump ring and seed bead. Create another strand with the other beads. Twist the two strands lightly around each other and secure to the toggle fastener or clasp.

MATERIALS

Polymer clay: Chocolate, Sahara,
various colours of green
Needle tool
Two black seed beads
30.5-cm (12-in.) length of thick
leather cording
Epoxy glue

PREPARATION

Marble Sahara and Chocolate
together to create a 5-cm (2-in.) long
tube bead. Poke a hole with cocktail
stick and leave inside the hole.

The monkey here appears to be swinging through the trees with no visible means of support – just like the real thing! The effect is created by building him around a cylindrical tube bead, through which you can thread the leather cord. As an extra twist, here we are also creating a toggle fastener in clay.

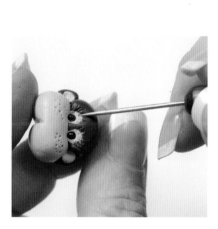

1 The hands are shaped from 5-mm (¼-in.) balls of Sahara flattened. Create an indentation with needle tool for the thumb. For the body, shape a 1-cm (½-in.) ball of Chocolate into a teardrop and elongate the neck area. Flatten a 5-mm (¼-in.) ball of Sahara and shape into a teardrop to add to the front of the body. For the feet, shape two 1.5-cm (⅝-in.) balls of Chocolate into teardrops. Round out the point of the teardrop and add tiny balls to for the toes. You can also add tinier balls of Sahara inside the toes for added detail. The head is a 1-cm (½-in.) Chocolate ball. Slightly flatten a 5-mm (¼-in.) Sahara ball into an oval and press onto the lower front of the face. Flatten two small Sahara balls and add to the face for eyes. Add two small Chocolate balls to the side of the head for ears.

2 Press in the eyes at the base of the Sahara-colour areas you added to the face in Step 1. Add detail marks to the face with the needle tool, using the photographs as a reference.

3 Assemble the pieces onto the cylinder bead. You want to give the appearance that he is hanging over the branch and holding on for dear life. Add additional detail with the needle tool. Add leaves, branches and beads strung on wire as desired, using the photograph as a guide.

4 Twist two strands of Chocolate clay together and wind around the end of the leather cord, then make a cross bar at the top. With another length, wind around the end of the leather cord again, but this time make a loop for the bar to fit through.

ASSEMBLING

Bake the monkey bead and the clay toggle without the cord in place. Allow to cool. Glue the ends of the leather cord inside the toggle pieces with 2-part epoxy glue.

CHAPTER 4

Millefiore Caning & Skinner Blend

Millefiore is a glass-working technique that has been adapted to use with polymer clay. The name literally means 'thousand flowers'. Creating canes can be time consuming at first, but it yields high rewards and canes can be stored, so you will soon develop a collection.

Think of caning like putting together a picture puzzle. Once you break down the various elements, the design is not overwhelming. Donna Kato, a well-known pioneer in polymer clay, has always been a source of inspiration. I thank her for teaching me many of these techniques, which I have tweaked a little to my own taste. As you work, you may find ways to add your own personal touch. The Skinner blend technique is another way of using colour, which is explained in detail on page 17. Here we put it into practise to create some amazing projects.

TRIBAL NECKLACE

There is something about this necklace that reminds me strongly of Africa. It may be the shapes, reminiscent of tribal necklaces, or perhaps the rich golden copper colour I have used. Of course, you do not have to use the same colours as I have – make the necklace to your own favourite shades, or to go with a particular outfit.

MATERIALS

Polymer clay: Black, Gold, Copper, Classic Translucent
Scrap clay
Polyblade
Pasta machine
Sandpaper block
Pro-bead roller set #2
Clear varnish
Beading wire
Two jump rings
Two crimp beads
Toggle fastener

1 Make a very large oval bead from a 2.5-cm (1-in.) ball of scrap clay. Pinch the ends to a point and flatten the sides roughly.

2 Shape the bead with your fingers into a triangular section tapering at the ends. The shape is thicker in the middle and pointed at each end.

3 Refine the shape you have made by rocking the polyblade gently around the base to smooth the curved edge.

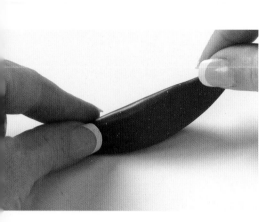

4 Rock the bead backwards and forwards on a flat surface to curve and smooth both the sides. Continue to refine the shape until you are happy with it.

5 Place the flat underside of the bead down on a sheet of Black clay rolled out on a medium setting on the pasta machine. Cut out around the bead.

6 Use a sandpaper block to add texture to the Black layer. This is just to give a finished look and you don't have to be concerned about fingerprints.

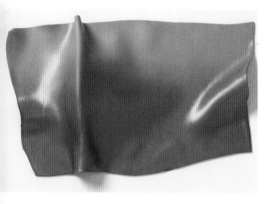

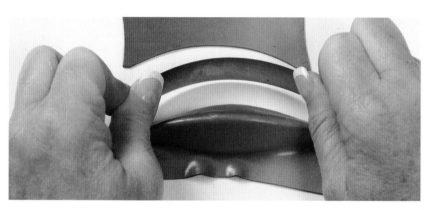

7 Create the Skinner blend with Copper and Gold, referring to the techniques section on page 17 to create the blend.

8 Lay the Skinner blend sheet over the pod bead. Use your fingers to smooth the sheet onto the bead, beginning at the top and working down. Cut off the excess sheet neatly along the edges by bending the polyblade around the curve of the shape.

9 Create a bull's-eye cane (see page 18) by wrapping a thin black sheet around a Classic Translucent log. Slice off thin sections of cane and add to the bead for decoration. Refer to the finished picture on page 103 for guidance on placement of the decorations. Put a cocktail stick through the end of the bead to make a hole for threading. Give the bead a final shape and smooth and wave the top edge. Make 11 pod beads and bake for one hour.

TIP
● The beads in this necklace are all similar in size, but you could make the centre one much bigger and grade the others down sharply in size on each side to give a nice curved effect to the front section of the necklace.

10 After baking, outline the top edge with a gold highlighting pen.

11 Sand the surface to smooth and buff on denim or apply varnish.

TIP
● *Add a drop of soap to the sandpaper, this keeps the clay particles from building up on the sandpaper and stops them from flying around in the air.*

ASSEMBLING

Create approximately 50 round copper beads using the pro-bead roller. Create holes with cocktail sticks and bake. Apply clear gloss varnish. Attach a jump ring to beading wire with a crimp bead. String on 17 copper beads, then add a copper bead between each pod bead. String on another 17 copper beads, finish with a jump ring and crimping bead. Attach the toggle fastener.

Variation: Pod Necklace

For a less chunky version, try this alternative idea. Make three beads as described in Steps 1–9, but make one around 5 cm (2 in.) long and the other two just over half that size. Do not make a hole right through the top as described in Step 9, instead make a hole in the very top of each bead for an eye pin. Make three round beads in the pro-bead roller, with a hole right through the centre. Bake all the beads.

Cut the eye pin down to around 5 mm (¼ in.) and thread on a round bead, then glue the eye pin into the top of the largest long bead. Repeat for the other two smaller beads. Attach the three beads to a fairly heavy chain using jump rings, with the largest in the centre and the two others spaced around 2.5 cm (1 in.) away on each side.

You could also use this technique to make matching earrings for both necklaces – make two extra of the smaller size beads and instead of adding them to the chain, attach them to a pair of earring wires.

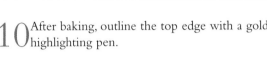

LOLLIPOP, LOLLIPOP

This luscious spiral bead looks good enough to eat – just like a real-life lollipop! I've hung it onto a plain silver chain, but you could string several together to make a very colourful and chunky necklace. The blended colours and curled shape look highly complex, but in fact this bead couldn't be easier to make.

MATERIALS

Polymer clay: Peppermint, White, Plum
Pasta machine
Polyblade
Log-shape base bead in scrap clay
Head pin
Two 2 mm Swarovski bi-cone crystals in co-ordinating colours
Silver chain

1 Flatten clay to the thickest setting of the pasta machine. Cut a triangle of each colour and arrange in a rectangle shape as shown.

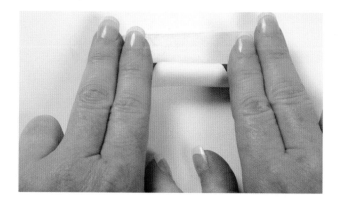

2 Instead of passing the rectangle through the pasta machine, roll the triangles up like you would to create a jellyroll.

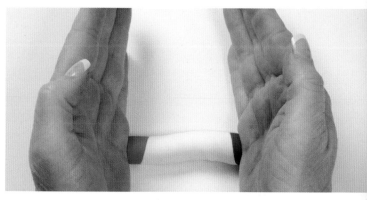

3 Compress the two ends of the roll gently but firmly in towards the centre between the base of the palms of your hands.

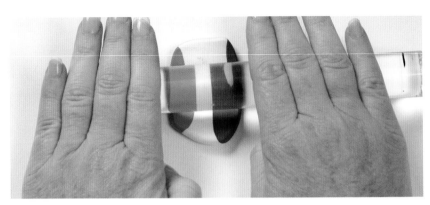

4 Keep compressing until the roll has been reduced to approximately 5 cm (2 in.) wide.

5 Flatten the roll out enough to get it through the pasta machine. Roll through the machine five times on the thickest setting. Note that the colour is on the sides.

6 Cut the flat clay sheet into a series of strips each around 1-cm (½-in.) wide.

7 Stack the strips on top of one another, then slice thin sections off with the polyblade.

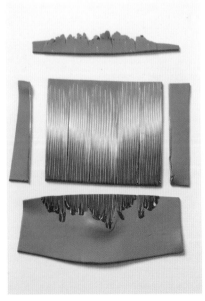

8 Flatten a sheet of Peppermint clay on a medium setting and lay the sections of pattern clay onto it. The backing makes it easier to wrap the clay around the bead. Set the pasta machine on the thickest setting and run the sheet through, gradually reducing the thickness to medium.

TIP
● Run the sliced sections through the pasta machine again after Step 7, beginning on the thickest setting and graduating down, to make sure they are an even thickness. Then place on the backing.

9 Trim off all four rough edges of the sheet to get a neat rectangle of the blending colours with no plain Peppermint showing.

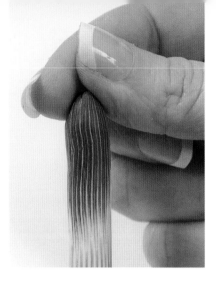

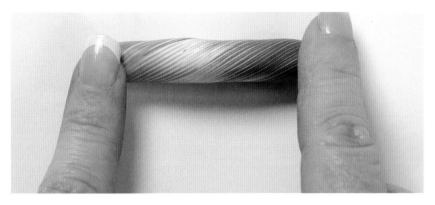

10 Wrap the sheet around a log-shaped base bead and shape the ends between your fingers.

11 Holding one side of the log, roll forwards with the opposite end, twisting the pattern. Continue to twist until you achieve a pleasing diagonal pattern.

12 Taper the ends of the bead to a point.

13 Roll the tapered bead up into a spiral.

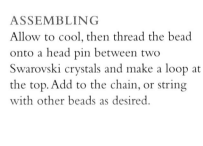

ASSEMBLING
Allow to cool, then thread the bead onto a head pin between two Swarovski crystals and make a loop at the top. Add to the chain, or string with other beads as desired.

14 Make a hole through the centre of the spiral with a cocktail stick and bake.

GEOMETRICS

Our eyes find geometric shapes very pleasing and black and tan goes with almost any outfit! Although this necklace looks complex, it's really only a combination of very simple canes. Make more beads than you think necessary and save them for other projects, or to assemble into the stretch bracelet for that quick gift!

MATERIALS

Polymer clay: Black, Sahara
Large round bead roller set
(optional)
Polyblade
Beading cord
Stretch cord

Necklace

PREPARATION

Roll Black and Sahara base beads using the bead roller or by hand – if you are going to cover the entire bead with patterned cane slices, use scrap clay so nothing goes to waste.

1 Roll the tan clay into a log 5 mm (¼ in) thick and 7.5 cm (3 in.) long. With the pasta machine on the third thinnest setting, roll a small sheet of Black clay. Lay the tan log on the sheet and bend the sheet around to wrap the log.

ASSEMBLING

Create holes in the beads with a cocktail stick and bake. Decide on the length of necklace you want and triple this measurement to allow for the cord taken up by knotting. Create a loop in one end of the cord and knot. String on a bead, push it close to the knot on the other side close to the bead. String on another and knot. Repeat until the necklace is complete. The last bead should slip through the loop made at the start and act as a fastener.

2 Using the polyblade, carefully trim off the excess Black clay where the ends of the sheet meet to neaten the ends of the strips.

3 Gently roll the cane back and forth, slightly stretching and elongating it until the log is 20 cm (8 in.) long. Using the polyblade, cut thin slices from the log. Refer to the basic caning technique section on pages 18–20 and build a variety of canes using Black and Sahara coloured clay – the more variety the better. Apply cane slices over the surface of the beads as desired.

Bracelet

For the bracelet, measure your wrist and add 5 cm (2 in.). String the beads onto a stretch cord and knot the ends together to finish. Clip off the excess cord and hide the knot in one of the beads. Chunky is funky!

CARNIVAL PARTY NECKLACE

The explosion of colour in this fun and funky necklace will be sure to get you noticed. Each of the beads is slightly different, but all are made using the same technique. Let your imagination run riot and try out different colour combinations.

MATERIALS

Polymer clay: Raspberry, Mandarin Orange, Peppermint, Pacific Blue, Plum, Sunflower Yellow, Tropical Green, Lime Green, White, Black

Scrap clay

Cocktail stick

Tube bead roller

Tri-bead roller

Bead stringing wire

24-gauge non-tarnish silver wire

Jump rings

Various silver accent beads

Head pins

Eye pins

3 mm round spacer beads

Two jump rings

Two crimp beads

Length of chain

Lobster clasp

TIP
● *This is a great project to use up all those odd ends of patterned cane and small pieces of clay leftover from other projects!*

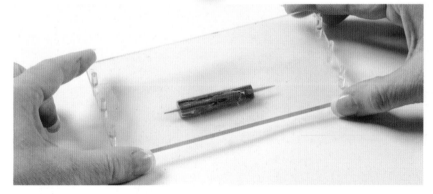

1 Using the techniques described on pages 18–20, make a variety of canes and striped blocks to choose from. Make a basic tube bead, and push a cocktail stick through the centre to make a hole for the wire.

2 Roll the bead in the tube bead roller with the cocktail stick still in place through the middle – this will keep the threading hole neat and even in shape as you reduce the bead itself down in size.

3 Cut the tube bead to the desired length with the polyblade. Slice off a thin section of striped block.

4 Pass the slice through the pasta machine on a thicker setting, graduating down to thin, to ensure that the section is one thickness. Wrap the bead.

5 Slice off a selection of bull's-eye patterns and use them to decorate the bead.

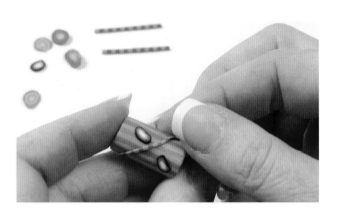

6 Add one or two striped strips diagonally, using the photograph as a guide. Add any additional decoration that you like.

7 Punch out small circles of plain colour clay to use to cap each end of the bead.

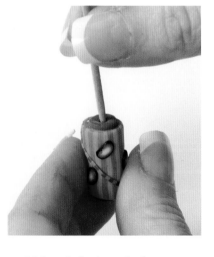

8 Add the circles to neatly cover the exposed raw ends of each of the beads.

9 Make a hole through the centre of the cap at each end to match the hole in the bead.

FINISHING

Repeat the above steps to create a variety of beads with different striped backgrounds and different canes to embellish them. You can also vary the length of the bead, making some long and others short. Create some solid colour round beads in assorted colours, using the tri-bead roller. Poke holes with cocktail sticks. Bake all beads.

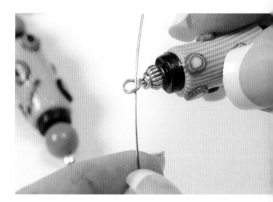

10 Thread a silver spacer bead onto a head pin, then a round bead, then the striped bead, round bead, spacer bead. Thread all the round beads onto head pins.

11 Using round-nose pliers, make a small loop in the end of each head pin. Repeat for all beads. Thread some on head pins and others on eye pins. Add dangle beads for the tube beads that have eye pins.

12 Cut a 25-cm (10-in.) length of beading wire and add a jump ring secured with a crimp bead. Thread on a round silver spacer, clay bead, round silver spacer, clay bead and repeat. Finish with a jump ring and crimp bead.

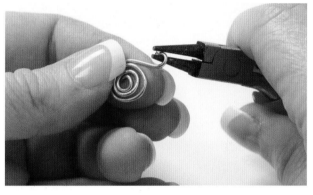

13 Create the spiral link in silver wire by using the round-nose pliers and creating a coil.

14 Loop the opposite end and attach to one end of a length of chain. Repeat for the other side.

TIPS

● *The patterns and colours used for these beads are random, but you could make several the same instead if you prefer. I personally like the exuberant effect of all the different colours and shapes!*

● *See the Carnival Bracelet on page 116 for further bead ideas to make in this style.*

ASSEMBLING

Open the jump rings and add them to the free ends of the chain. Attach the lobster clasp to the chain ends.

CARNIVAL BRACELET

This bracelet uses the same canes and colours as the Carnival Party Necklace on page 113, but here the beads are oval and round, instead of tubes. However, you can make the two pieces to match as an ensemble, if you prefer. Remember you do not have to use the same colours as here – try following this idea but in co-ordinating colours instead.

MATERIALS

Polymer clay: Raspberry, Mandarin Orange, Peppermint, Pacific Blue, Plum, Sunflower Yellow, Tropical Green, Lime Green, White, Black

Scrap clay

Pro-bead roller #2

Tri-bead roller

Cocktail stick

Memory wire

Memory wire shears

Round-nose pliers

> *TIP*
> ● *When you are squeezing the wrapped stripes at the end of the bead, work slowly and evenly around the top so the stripes will converge nicely into the centre. Cover the last bit with a cap in a contrasting colour.*

1 Using the techniques described on pages 18–20, make a variety of canes and striped blocks to choose from. Create the base beads from scrap clay using the pro-bead roller. Take a pinch of clay out of the base bead to allow for adding the wrapped clay. Roll the bead into a log and wrap the striped sheet around the basic bead shape.

2 Pinch the ends of the bead together gently with your fingers, working around until the gap in the cover at each end of the bead is closed and the stripes cover the entire bead.

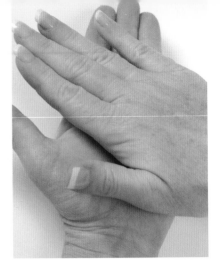

3 Put the striped bead back into the bead roller and gently roll it again to smooth and re-shape it.

4 To make the large round bead, cover a base bead as described above, then roll the bead between the palms of your hands to form it into a large ball.

5 The bead does not have to be perfectly even and you can make a variety of shapes.

6 Slice thin sections from some of your basic canes and dot them around all the different striped beads.

7 Make two small round beads with your fingers, flatten slightly and apply to each end of the large round bead.

8 Make a hole right through the centre of each bead with a cocktail stick, using the technique described on page 15. Create basic black round beads with the tri-bead roller. Poke a hole through with a cocktail stick and bake all the beads.

TIPS

● Using memory wire means that the bracelet will curl around your wrist naturally in several loops, so you will not need a fastener for this project.

● If you prefer you could link the beads with short lengths of chain for a more open effect. Try out some of your own ideas to get a really unique look!

● Don't forget that you should never cut memory wire with ordinary cutters as it will damage the blade. Invest in proper memory wire cutters or shears if you wish to use this material.

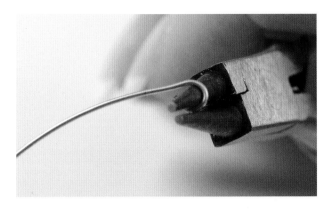

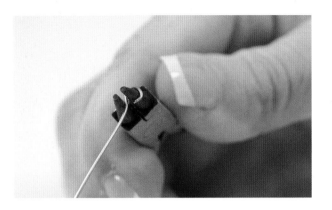

9 Using memory wire shears, cut a length of memory wire that will give you approximately three loops around your wrist. Using round-nose pliers, bend the end of the wire to form a loop.

10 Twist the loop back the other way slightly, so that the circle you have just made is centred on the length of wire.

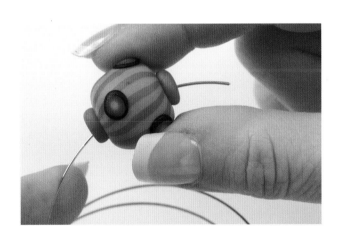

11 Thread the beads onto the wire with black beads between each caned bead. Finish with a loop. As an option, you may want to add a little dangle from each loop.

Variation: Charm Bracelet

If you do not want to use the memory wire, these gloriously vibrant beads can also be made up into an unusual 'charm' bracelet.

Make the beads in exactly the same way as described for this project. Thread a small spacer bead onto a head pin, add a finished bead then another spacer bead. Twist the top of the head pin into a loop, as described in Steps 9–10 above. Cut off the excess wire. Use a jump ring to attach each bead dangle onto a chain bracelet, spacing them out around its length.

Remember that you can vary the size and the shape of your beads for this bracelet, just as the charms may often vary quite widely in size on the original version.

VICTORIAN FLOWERS

This is perhaps the most complex project in the book, but don't let that frighten you! If you have worked your way through some of the other projects and got the hang of working with polymer clay, you will find the basic techniques used here easy – all I have done is used several all together in one project.

MATERIALS

Polymer clay: Plum, White, Tropical Green, Lime Green, Black
Pasta machine
Polyblade
Pro-bead roller #2
Tri-bead roller
Swarovski bi-cone crystals
Cocktail sticks
Twenty-nine eye pins
Gloss varnish
Gold leafing pen
Large silver chain links
Twenty jump rings
Toggle fastener

TIP
● *You can make other types of flower using the same basic technique – study a gardening book or seed catalogues for inspiration on shape and colours to try.*

PREPARATION

Create a Skinner blend roll using Plum and White for the flower, following the instructions on page 20. Make another Skinner blend roll from Tropical and Lime Green for the leaves.

1 To make the flower cane, stand the Skinner blend cane on end and cut it in half lengthways.

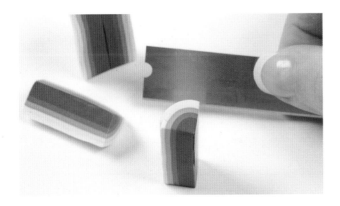

2 Cut each half cane in half again lengthways, so you now have four canes that are a quarter circle or quadrant shape.

3 Flatten the quarters, moving the White edge upwards round towards the Plum.

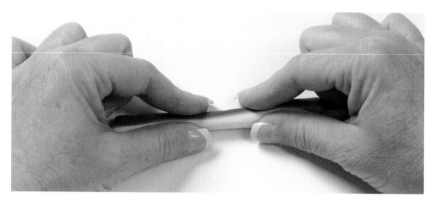

4 Stack the four re-shaped pieces together as shown.

5 Stretch and pull the stack you have just made from the centre, working to double its length.

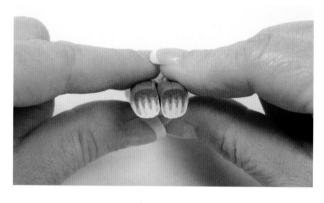

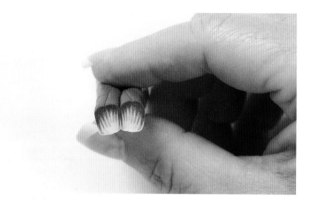

6 Cut the stack in half and put two the halves together side by side, as shown.

7 Stretch and pull again from the centre, working to double the length.

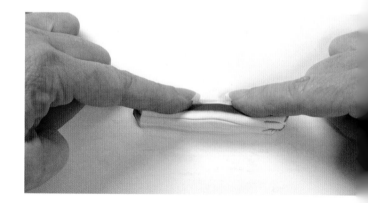

8 Cut in half and put two halves together side by side, as shown.

9 Press in at the bottom, darker end to make a teardrop or petal shape.

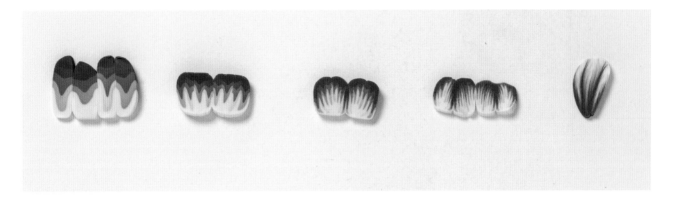

10 This sequence shows the progression of the shapes through all the steps.

TIP
● Make more flower and leaf cane than you will need for the main focal bead, as you will use it again for the smaller beads. You can store any spare as described on page 10, to use for future projects.

11 To make the leaves, use the green Skinner cane. Cut the log into three equal sections.

12 Take out the middle section and place it flat side down onto a sheet of Black clay rolled to the thinnest setting on the pasta machine. Cut out around the sides of the log.

13 Add another thin sheet of Black to the top of the middle section log and trim off the excess clay flush with the sides.

14 Place the pieces back together so the log now has two parallel black lines running through it.

15 Turn the log so that the black lines are on a diagonal and make a slice through the centre.

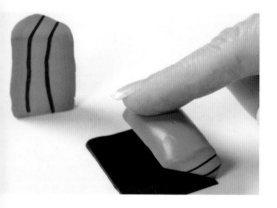

16 Add a thin sheet of Black clay to one flat side of one half of the cane.

17 Turn the other piece of cane around and place the two halves back together.

18 Wrap around the outer edge of the cane with a thin layer of Black.

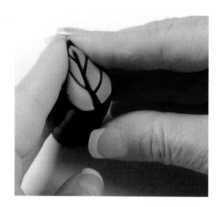

19 Shape the cane into a leaf shape. Stretch and pull to reduce the cane in size, reducing one end to grade the cane and get different size leaves when you slice.

20 Make a large oval bead in Black clay, using the pro-bead roller. make eight smaller oval beads and six round Black beads with the tri-bead roller.

21 Slice off several thin leaves in different sizes from your leaf cane and add them to the large bead using the photograph as a guide.

22 Add around six of the larger petals in a circle over the top of the leaves, to make a fairly large flower shape. Press gently to attach them securely.

23 Add a second circle of smaller petals in the centre of the flower. Place a crystal in the centre of the flower and push it in gently to embed it.

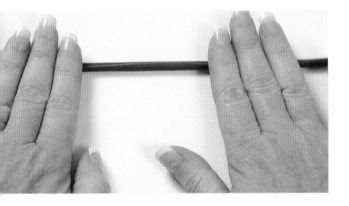

24 Take the remainder of your flower cane and roll and stretch it some more until it has quadrupled in length.

25 Cut the roll into four sections. Put three together and add a thin yellow log in the centre. Add the final petal to the last side.

FINISHING

Poke holes through all the beads. Add an eye pin to the top of the focal bead, then bake all the beads. Allow to cool and apply gloss varnish. Daub gold leaf pen onto a ceramic tile to form a puddle of gold. Use a cocktail stick to pick up gold and paint outlines on the beads. You can also embellish and fill in areas with gold dots.

26 Slice flowers from this cane and add to the smaller oval beads. Add leaves.

ASSEMBLING

Thread a crystal, bead, crystal onto each remaining eye pin and loop the top. Using the photograph of the necklace as your guide, attach the loops to the large chain links as desired. Add the toggle fastener.

Templates

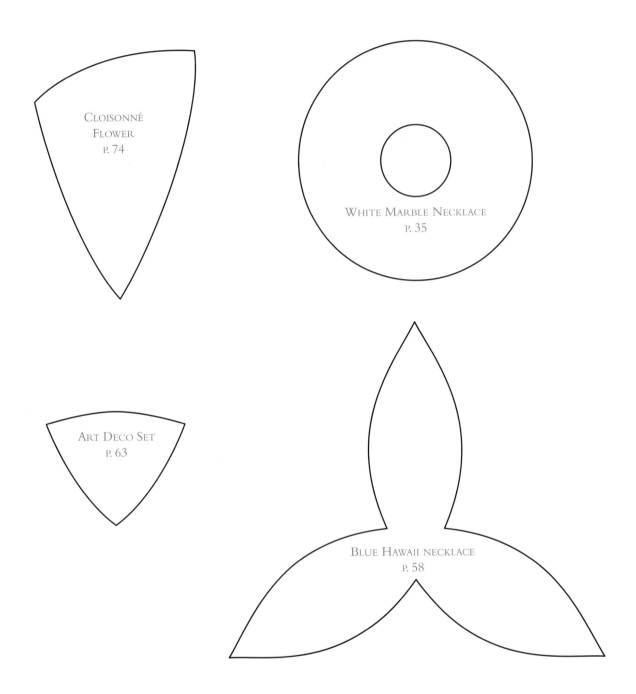

Cloisonné
Flower
p. 74

White Marble Necklace
p. 35

Art Deco Set
p. 63

Blue Hawaii necklace
p. 58

Resources and Suppliers

LINDA PETERSON, DESIGNER ARTIST:
www.lindapetersondesigns.com
www.lindapetersondesigns.blogspot.com
email:
lindapetersondesigns@yahoo.com

Products

FIMO SOFT AND FIMO CLASSIC
POLYMER CLAY, FIMO GEL:
Eberhard Faber/Fimo
www.fimo.com

PASTA MACHINE, BEAD ROLLERS,
BEAD BAKING RACK, BEAD MAKING
TOOLS, ARTEMBOSS PEWTER METAL,
PEEL OFF OUTLINE SPECIALTY
STICKERS, EASY METAL SILVER AND
GOLD LEAFING SHEETS:
Amaco
www.amaco.com
(001) 317-244-6871

UK Stockist:
All About Crafts
www.allaboutcrafts.com
+44 (0)1782 745000

ADIRONDAK ALCOHOL INKS,
MELTING POT, UTEE, UTEE FLEX:
Ranger Industries
www.rangerink.com
(001) 732-389-3535

UK Distributor of Ranger Products:
Personal Impressions
www.personalimpressions.com
+44 (0)1787 375241

BEADING WIRE, LEATHER CORDING,
CRIMP BEADS, JEWELRY TOOLS:
Beadalon
www.beadalon.com
(001) 610-466-6000

DARK T-SHIRT TRANSFERS/DECALS:
Avery Dennison Corp
www.avery.com
(001) 800-462-8379

PEARL EX MICA POWDERS:
Jacquard Inc
www.jacquardproducts.com,
(001) 800-442-0455

NON TARNISH SILVER AND
COPPER WIRES:
Artistic Wire
www.artisticwire.com,
(001) 610-466-6000

ARTFUL RUBBER STAMPS:
PaperArtsy
www.paperartsy.co.uk
+44 (0)1277 212911

POLYMER CLAY STAMPING MATS:
ClearSnap
www.clearsnap.com
(001) 360 293-6634

GOLD LEAFING PEN:
Krylon
www.krylon.com

MISCELLANEOUS SPACER AND
GLASS BEADS:
Blue Moon Beads
www.bluemoonbeads.com
(001) 866-404-7640

Halcraft
www.halcraft.com
(001) 914-840-0505

FANTASY FIBRES:
Art Institute Glitter
www.artglitter.com
(001) 928-639-0805

FOLK ART AND APPLE BARREL
ACRYLIC PAINT:
Plaid Industries
www.plaidonline.com
(001) 800-842-4197

Acknowledgements

I am blessed to have been surrounded by other talented polymer clay artists who have given me so much in the way of inspiration. I would like to thank Donna Kato, my friend and mentor, who has helped open numerous doors for me in this industry, Christi Friesen, an artist whose work I've admired for a long time and who inspired the sculpted section of the book, and Karen Lewis, aka Klew. The first time I saw Karen's beads at a trade show, I fell in love with beading – her work is so intricately exquisite. I'd like to thank her particularly for inspiring the Ivory Coast necklace.

Index